Enjoy
Karen Peter

Spirit Adventures

Spirit Adventures

A Medium's Memoir -Interactions with Spirits- Private Cases in the Paranormal

Karen Tatro

Published by Tablo

Publisher and wholesale enquiries: orders@tablo.io

20 21 22 23 LSC 10 9 8 7 6 5 4 3 2 1

Table of Contents

Special Thanks to my super supportive family!

Thank you to my incredibly supportive family, who have not only encouraged me to explore, embrace and fully honor my gifts, but for all the sacrificing of my personal time that I have devoted to my work as a medium.

I love you all so much and truly hope that my journey in the spirit world has inspired and helped each of you along your own way in life.

Thank you to my clients who have reached out to me for assistance in your homes and businesses. I am forever bonded to you all!

And to the Spirits that reside…
"We are all Spiritual Beings, living a Human Life"

Life Purpose

"When I let go of what I Am, I become what I might Be"
Lao Tzu

Preface

Karen and her dog Spanky

So, it has been quite a journey these past 10 years, as I sit here in my sunroom and begin this process of writing about my spirit adventures. It has been such an incredible journey, one that I am forever grateful for. How did this all begin? Well, the funny thing about it, is that this was never something that I really set out to do, or to be, it just happened one crazy weekend at a haunted hotel. What happened exactly? Well, it was when the reality of my life's purpose on some level was really revealed to me. It was that moment of really coming to terms with my mediumship abilities. Everyone always asks me what it is like being a medium and boy I guess I have to answer that by saying, and I add a little humor here, it depends on what phase of my life I was in to best answer that question. As a child I was quite accepting of my; "Karenisms" as many who know me refer to that terminology sometimes to best describe those moments of "me".

Mom and Dad at their prom

My childhood was much like many, two very loving and wonderful parents. My mom and dad were young when they had me and truly describe our childhood as growing up together. Learning what it was like to be parents at the age of 17 and having to figure out not only being a parent, but also a parent of a child who saw spirits and was in touch with the spirit world and things unseen. We lived in Arizona, which was a magical place for me on so many levels. I was always the kid that played outside and "talked" to the trees and land as if they were my "friends". I loved being in Arizona and have such great memories of my time, playing in the riverbed near our trailer and having adventures of my own. I had imaginary friends and had insights that truly just were of my own. My parents were not really into spirituality, heck they were trying to figure out how to be teenagers and parents. My father was a talented musician and artist on the verge of signing a record deal and playing back up for the Rolling Stones and the Mama and Papa's, while my mom was a nurse trying to also balance her passion for wanting to be a doctor and now approaching the reality that she was going to be a single mother. Yah, my parents separated and that was devastating for me and a book all on its own.

Me and my Dad

I can recall the instance of playing outside in the riverbed and somehow managed to sit on a prickly pear cactus. You can imagine the pain I was experiencing while my parents were trying to remove the hundreds of thorns from my behind and my "Karenism" of being more worried that I killed the cactus and was it okay? I laugh when I think of this, because that was my world, everything was alive, and everything was my "friend". That was me and it continued in my life, along with my stubborn sense of needing to do things on my own and be my own person. Teaching myself to swim and refusing, sometimes screaming at all the people in the community pool in Arizona to leave me alone and I will figure it out myself. As I type this, I think, my poor parents. Ha, ha. But that was me and all was good in my land of imagination and exploration.

One of my fondest real encounters was when I was probably around 7 or 8 and was watching TV alone in the living room. I had this feeling and sensation, like something calling me to go to my bedroom which was shared with my younger sister, Kendra. My bedroom door was ajar, and a bright light was illuminated from the room. As I approached and opened the door, there stood this huge, glowing figure of a woman, just totally engulfed in swirling beautiful colors, much like how we may describe an angelic being. There she was, this beautiful female, smiling at me. The amount of love and peace coming from her was so amazing to ever be able to describe with words. In that moment though, what I remember is that I felt like I was seeing my friend and looked up at her and smiled back, this exchange of "knowing" between the two of us. I then just went back to the living room and continued to watch TV, like no big deal. I just saw this amazing apparition or angelic being, and went back to watching TV, yah, that is exactly what happened. It was not anything to be afraid of if anything it was a "hello again" moment. As I type this, it makes me think of this beautiful female voice that often comes in when I do my readings. There are times that I deliver more channeled messages to my clients and often for myself. They are messages that I have often written down, as they are so incredibly wise. Who she is exactly, I do not presume to even know or try to know, just that she has been a higher presence in my life for as far as I can remember? I will enclose some of her messages at the end of this book. Hopefully, her words of wisdom that have truly touched me and many of my clients, will also touch something inside of you.

As I grew in my life, like many of us do, there was this awareness that I had knowing and could not really understand and figure them out. We did not have the internet, libraries, TV shows or people openly talking about spirits and the unknown. We had the TV show, In Search Of and boy did I watch that. I was fascinated by the stories of the unknown, Bigfoot and UFOs. I was convinced that Bigfoot was outside my window each night, ready to eat me. I do recall though that this time of life, between ages 10-12, I began to feel a sense of fear with spirits and would wake up each night terrified. I had many visitors at night, spirits standing in my room talking to me, trying to get my attention and what seemed as passed people needing something from me. This was not the best time in my life for this, as there was no one really to help me understand why these spirits were visiting me and how to not only stop it but at least be able to work with it. It was also an exceedingly difficult time in my childhood with a lot of trauma from my parents' divorce. I can recall on many occasions being woken and scared out of my mind, hearing people calling my name and talking to me, which would then result in me wetting the bed. I would stand in the hallway with my stepfather, as my mom worked nights at this time and ask him if he heard them, with the usual reply of let's get your bed made and get back to bed.

As with many things in life, we fear what we do not understand and as a kid, that time when our rational mind begins to develop, we are sort of in the in-between. The reality is that hold on a minute, our imaginary friends are not real, and mermaids do not exist? I never grew out of this ability as many children can, but more so did not entertain or embrace it much anymore. This began the time when TV began to enlighten me to the darker side of it all. I saw the Exorcist when I was just 12 years old and truly that movie freaked me out, as with many people, I'm sure that was not the best thing for me at such a vulnerable and impressionable time in my life. It was fascinating on one hand, just as Bigfoot, Aliens, and the Loch Ness Monster were, but this was REAL! This was a real story of a child possessed. I had nightmares and imagined these voices I heard, surely would not be good.

In most of my adult life, now that I think of it, even in the time of adolescence, I woke up often to having visitors in my room. It is just the strangest feeling to explain to people. It begins with my body, sensing something in the room before I am even awake. I wake to feeling that adrenaline growing in me and the clammy feeling much like what many of us women feel as a hot flash or maybe what many may feel as an anxiety attack. I realize that, okay, something is in the room and I am a little scared to open my eyes. I lay there for a moment with my eyes shut and feel like my heart is going to jump right out of my chest. It is an awfully familiar feeling that I have experienced time and time again. So, what do I do, but have to open my eyes and deal with it, but for me at this time, it is more just opening my eyes, and acknowledging you are there and then realize with my rational mind, okay you're not real. Then they go away. Looking back, I also now understand that many of these spirits more than likely were people that were coming to me because they could sense this ability that I had. They may have wanted me to possibly help them or pass on messages to their loved ones? Ghee, did they know ahead of time this would be my calling eventually and would not be fearful of it. My son and I talk about this reality now in my adult life, how we all have "timelines" so to speak, he calls them. I call them the "windows" of our knowing, and truthfully with all time being eternal in that spirit realm, just maybe they were there to sort of show me where I was going when ready? I also have understood that some of these visits were my spirit guides and those that walk with me in this lifetime.

I can recall many times seeing a man hovering, sitting Indian style by my bed, looking at me with a book in his hand and talking to me with words of wisdom. He was dressed as what we may referred to as a monk, or Tibetan man. How funny that for years now, he often comes in during my readings to help assist people sitting with me. But how would I have known that growing up if I did not eventually just face my fears and the ridicule of being "Phoebe" on friends as I was often referred to in my family and friends' group. Even though I feel extremely far from Phoebe, but yes, I do have those "Karenisms" and I guess that makes sense.

So let's fast forward a bit, as this is not an autobiography but more so briefly moving through the development I guess of my "Karenisms" and getting to the work that I currently do, which is the world of Ghosts and Spirits.

I like many could write an autobiography about all the different spirit experiences in my life and much about many things, however, I really wanted to bring you sort of down a road that led me to this embracing. As I grew, of course I had many profound encounters and moments of really beginning to understand this all, but nothing truly was as powerful as the time in my life that was face to face with my fears and the reality of just what I was; a medium.

The Mirror Magazine

In 2009, I decided with much probing that I really wanted to bring my abilities to a place of not only understanding them, but to fully embrace them and well, honor that inner knowing that I have this for a reason. I created a digital magazine, The Mirror Magazine. It was a simple magazine of maybe 66 pages, all detailing pictures, articles and stories of spirituality and paranormal. I thought, okay this is the perfect place to start to talk about these topics. This would be a common ground, a place of discussion and a place where I could share my experiences, thoughts and feelings about these topics but also research and interview people in the field. It was not a very profitable adventure for me, but it covered itself. I learned how to become a graphic artist and magazine publisher, all on my own. It is something that to this day I am still proud of myself for deciding to do and figured it out all on my own and without any college degree or backing to do so. One of the many lectures I give to people, that truly if you want to do something, there really is a will and a way to do it. Often, we must be our own inspiration, motivator and parent in many ways, or we will never achieve our goals and dreams.

Literary Award

In my May addition, I wanted to feature a haunted hotel and what it would be like to personally spend the night at a haunted hotel. I was going to write about my experiences along with others who have stayed at a haunted hotel. I thought this would be a great article and would also open the doors to exploring the field, for my own personal reasons. Boy,

I had no idea what the future would reveal for me and the path that it would lead me down. It did not just open a door for me, it really opened the floodgates as they say. It changed my life and became still to this day one of the most profound spirit experiences that I had.

So, this is where it all began for me; The Shanley Hotel in Napanock NY, in 2010.

I will share with you my story of the Shanley Hotel along with other locations, both public and private cases that I have worked on over the past 10 years in this series. Everything you will read will be true encounters and my personal insights regarding the spirit world. I have learned a great deal in all my encounters. One thing that I have always prided myself on, is the fact that all my wisdom and much of what I teach or talk about truly is from the spirits I encounter; my readings, galleries, cases and events, and not from a book or other people's insights.

There is a great deal of living to learn from the spirits on the other side! As I always say, Spirituality and Paranormal co-exist together and we are all spiritual beings living a human life.

So, enjoy and thank you for going on this journey with me.

Karen Tatro Spirit Medium

The Shanley Hotel

Napanock, NY
2010

Shanley Hotel

I will never forget the anxiety of making the decision to go to the Shanley Hotel. I went back and forth with this decision, for so many reasons. I had a bit of fear, an OMG moment of am I really going to do this? Am I really going to subject myself to the very thing that I often have been afraid of? What made me choose the Shanley Hotel to be the first place I would go and write about? Well, when I decided to go to a hotel, I began reaching out to other people on Facebook in regards to my magazine; The Mirror Magazine, in ways of researching and looking for articles to write in reference to paranormal teams, equipment and experiences that people were having. I can't say exactly how it all transpired but a few very interesting things began to occur and the notion that spirits call out to you and perhaps even visit you is something I learned later on to be as real as knowing my name. It brings me back to my childhood and the many nights waking up with visitors in my room. Now I have a little more understanding of just why that occurred.

There was some discussion with a paranormal group about this hotel in Napanock, NY. A Facebook friend from a team in NJ, had posted that it was the real deal! He posted a few pictures of the hotel, both exterior and interior photos that showed this classic rundown haunted looking hotel that claimed to have over 33 known spirits haunting it. The pictures were intriguing for sure. A huge rundown white building with peeling paint and broken windows, more so looking abandoned that open for business. The interior pictures looked like Victorian era décor with rich drapery and stenciled walls, vibrant colors and an old antique flare about it.

This investigator said it was the Real Deal! So, with that being said, I reached out to him. I was not fully sure what I was reaching out for exactly. Yes, I was wanting to know what he had felt there and if he recommended it for my article. I had not known that I was a "medium" at this time. So, the idea of going to an extremely haunted hotel with 33 known ghosts wandering the halls, well, the thought that I may be just nuts, was in the back of my mind. I shit you not! He advised me that it was great and that I should go.

It is hard to imagine the whole concept of going to a haunted hotel. After all, this was not something that I fully was embracing and just started to explore the whole notion that I needed to conquer my fear. But on this day, I looked up the site and after seeing the first welcome page, thought okay this looks neat.

At first, I went on the website a few random times, just looking at the rooms and exploring some of the different tabs it had for visiting. There was this part of me that was drawn to the hotel and afraid of it, all at the same time. I can't really explain it totally, but I guess maybe like standing at the end of a diving board and you are drenched in sweat on a hot summer day and you see the water below, looking so refreshing and welcoming. You want to just jump in and feel the coolness, but you are a bit afraid of heights and the jump seems a bit much. Oh, the struggle begins!

I must have gone on and off that site for the entire day, and then the thought of omg, who is going to go with me because there is no way I am going alone. The funny thing is that generally, I would rather go alone, often my best self is when I am exploring things on my own, less distractions. But for some reason, this time it was sort of heading out on unknown waters so to speak and felt I must have someone go.

At the time, my best friend; Heather was more than excited to go. She was the friend that really nudged me to explore my spiritual ways, or "Karenism's" as we say. Meeting Heather that particular year was life changing for me in many ways. First in that as I stated earlier, I have really kept my spirit experiences and knowing to myself. It is hard to really share this insight, wisdom and confusions with anyone that this does not happen to. I can understand now looking back how hard it was for my family and husband to fully understand, even though they wanted to, it was hard for them. I am sure that it would be the same for anyone that is into science and trying to talk about all the stuff that is going on in their head, to an English major. It is a part of you that needs to be stimulated and explored but impossible without the right receptive people. If you don't get it, you just don't get it.

Heather was the first person in a long time, and well, at the time the only person that I could really talk to about all the crazy spirit stuff going on in my mind. I met Heather when our son's played school baseball together and one day, she overheard me talking about something, and to this day I still don't really know what it was, but she came up to me and we just started talking. Our friendship just grew from there. It was a bit of a mind-blowing experience for me, I have to say, because I started to talk about my experiences and thoughts and omg she was so receptive to listen but also was getting it and had a lot of her own things to share. It seriously was like my soul sister had just flown into my life to ignite this spiritual fire.

She was feeling the same way in her life and really for the most part, we had similar lives. We each had 2 kids, and a husband who we adore and love, but just does not get this part of us. My "Karenism's and her "Heatherland". How funny is that. Our family had names for our ways. My husband often describes it as the "butterfly effect" when you see a butterfly and you can be totally engulfed in a conversation and here comes along a butterfly. The butterfly grabs your attention and off you go, lost in a totally other direction. "Karen, hello?" This is how it is and for anyone what does any kind of spiritual work with me, you already know those moments for me. Ha!

So here I am at this point with a new friend and we began to just encourage each other to explore our full self. So many times, in my work I have described the feeling with people that you really do have 2 aspects of yourself. You have your human side, and we all know this side. This is the side that functions in the world of material. We have families, responsibilities, ambitions and jobs, which all require a certain amount of focus and drive to succeed in the world and all we do. But we also have our spirit or soulful self and that is something that many people do not always give attention to. It is easy to get caught up in the human ways of living and forget to take care of our soulfulness. That childlike quality we use to have. To play and have fun and laugh out loud and take risks and adventures just for fun. Often when we are not feeding our soul, as they say, well, we can become a bit lost inside. On the outside all may be simply great, but inside something is missing.

This was something that my friend, Heather and I were experiencing in our lives. Happiness in many ways but also a bit of a restless, uneasy feeling that we were not truly fully embracing this spiritual quirkiness we have. One of the greatest things about my friendship with Heather was that for once in a long time I had met someone that saw in me what I always saw and wanted to help bring that out. Our friendship was not all about me being her therapist or motivator but more so equal in that I was to inspire her as much as she was to inspire me. One of the things that she inspired and pushed me to do was to explore my writing by sharing my experiences and abilities with those who would benefit by knowing me. Hence, where the Mirror Magazine took its roots.

The Mirror Magazine was a digital magazine that I created in 2009-2010. It was truly created by my own vision and a place to share both paranormal and spiritual insights, wisdom and education with the public. I wanted to share both my own experiences and share everyone else's experiences. I felt it was a safe and neutral platform to begin with. I had no idea that it would also be the catalyst for many things in my life.

Shanley Hotel

Creating the magazine and learning how to be a graphic artist and work with a highly advanced graphic program, was a new experience. I could write a whole chapter just on this topic alone. It truly taught me that it does not matter what education or knowledge you have, there is always room to learn and most certainly can do anything you truly put your mind and passion to do. I learned how to do things that I had never in a million years thought I could do.

The magazine allowed me the adventure not only to write, which was always a passion of mine, but to also get a bit of exposure in a field that I was just beginning to explore. So, I designed my first issue to be published May 1st of 2010 and partly based on my experiences at a haunted hotel. I was going to write about my own journey there, and a bit about the history of the hotel. It was truly going to be my featured article.

So here I am, totally ready to set sail and now all I need is someone to go with me and Heather was on board. We both were continually drawn to the imagery of the hotel. It was nicely displayed on the welcome page, a huge white 3 story massive building with paint peeling, boards slightly rotted and well, to be honest, sort of teetered on the abandoned creepy looking building. It had its appeal as being a truly haunted looking building just looking at the photo.

Blue Room (Mr. Roosevelt often stayed in this room}

Entrance Staircase

What really drew me in, was a few pictures of the entrance stairs. They were rich with dark mahogany, Victorian patterned wallpaper with bold colors and vibrant red trim work. Just looking at the staircase made you want to walk up them. There was one photo of one of the Victorian rooms. The room appeared to bring you back in time, a time where you would imagine a female sitting in her white Victorian room. The room displayed a delicate, beautiful dresser and large full-length mirror. The curtains and bedspread all elegant white lace. I could just imagine a woman sitting at the dresser putting her hair up and getting herself ready for the day or evenings social gathering. This room completely drew me in. I wanted to sleep in that room and sit in that very spot, stepping back in time. Little did I know that room was calling to me.

The room was not the only thing calling me, the hotel's occupants were also calling to me. I can remember waking up at night dreaming of the hotel and oddly knowing that someone was in my room disturbing my sleep, which was not uncommon for me in my life. I can recall my entire life being woken up by the feeling that someone was visiting. It would always start with that six-sense feeling as many describe the goosebumps, cold sweats and heart racing to slowly open my eyes afraid of what I may see. Sure, enough as I open my eyes there would be someone standing in my room looking at me. Most of my life this was frightening, and it would make me so uneasy. As a kid, I would often quickly pull the blankets over my head and in my adult life before I fully embraced this all, I would just roll over and pray they would go away. Now in my life, as I embraced the ability and do the work, I truly understand that many of these spirits were people reaching out to me and some maybe trying to get a message to their family and also my own spirit guides delivering messages to me. I am amazed how over time and the work I do; I sleep peacefully and not disturbed anymore. I think my spirit guides have become my bodyguards to some degree and realize that I work hard doing this spirit work and given myself to others that they make sure I get a good night sleep. I swear I can hear them, "give the girl a break". Sounds funny as I type this, but it truly seems to be the case.

So, as I look back, I recall those visits prior to going to the hotel. I also recall one of the strangest events happening that completely validated the hotel was calling me. If you recall reading earlier that one of my contacts in the paranormal groups had told me about the hotel originally. His name was Ron. He had messaged me a few times about the hotel and said to go check it out as it was the "real deal", his exact words. We were just Facebook friends and honestly really did not correspond a lot. I saw one day that I had an inbox message from him. I of course opened the message and here was this old newspaper clipping of a story about the Shanley Hotel. It was incredibly old and hard to read, but showed what seemed to be a quick story about the hotel's owners and a picture of a few men looking very much back in the 1800's. I feel awful that I do not recall what the article was about as it was very hard to read. I was having doubts about going to the hotel, my fear factor kicked in prior to getting this article as Heather had said she was not able to come with me, so at this time it meant going alone. So, suddenly as I am in doubt about going, here shows up this article. I remember opening it and reading what I could and then messaged Ron a big thank you for the message and that I was going to go and not let fear keep me from going. To my surprise, Ron messaged me back and said, "Karen, I didn't send you an article." I was a bit dumbfounded and questioned him, but he swears he did not send me that article and as I went back to look for it, it was gone. As I am typing this, I think I am going to scroll through my messages from him and see if I can find it, just for old times' sake.

So here is this article that showed up in my inbox on its own? Okay, I guess I must go. Shanley is calling me and there must be a reason! As I go forward with this, I can tell you that there was, and it forever changed me and my view of life.

What next? We go! I thought to myself, okay, so here you are packing up for the weekend trip to the Shanley Hotel. My companion was a good friend and ex-sister in law at the time, Colleen Brown. She was eager and ready to go explore with me.

Sal Nicosia; Owner of Shanley

I reached out to the owner of the hotel, Sal Nicosia. A tear in my eye as I type. Sal had his own part of truly helping my soul in ways that I can never fully express to anyone. Much like Heather, Sal was also someone that was truly a part of this soulful journey into the depth of my being that the only way I can really describe it is to imagine that your whole life, or at least to this point in your life, you have no one in your life that truly validates, accepts and helps you embrace yourself, up until this point, yes family, friends love you and care about you but they don't understand and in many ways ridicule your ways from time to time. Then people cross your path and are your soulful warriors who completely get it, and not only do they get it, they motivate you to be all you are and all you were meant to be in this life. It heals you deeply and you become connected to them in deep ways. When someone tells you, you are sane when you have been wondering about your sanity for years. Just imagine that! That is the best way to describe it.

I reached out to Sal and he was eager and willing to welcome me to write about the hotel in my magazine. He let me come free of charge to stay at the hotel and write about my experiences. What I loved is that he was the most down to earth person I think I had ever met at this time in my life. He related in many ways, as Sal had never considered himself a paranormal or spiritual person, with abilities and such that he welcomed or even embraced. He was a businessman to some degree. He had told me that he purchased the run-down hotel with all good intentions of making a profit. The building was vacant and desolate in the small town of Napanock, NY. There the massive white abandoned building stood on Main street, run down, paint peeling without anyone interested in buying the old hotel. The hotel that once was a thriving magnificent grand hotel in its day. That we will get to in a bit, but this was a building that the town was seriously considering tearing down, from what Sal had told me. So, he bought it and had grand intentions of restoring the hotel back to its glory with a nice profitable for sale sign. He was a man who had the means to do the work and begin the construction and rebuilding the hotel. What a task, he described as it was in the condition to mainly be gutted and stripped down to bare bones, to then start over.

The hotel sort of spiritual called to him, he told me. He often passed by the hotel as he had another home, he had restored just a block away. It was known as the "Stone House" and Sal and his wife; Cindy restored this beautiful home from the ashes to glory, landing them a full article in a prestigious magazine. As he drove by the hotel, he felt that pull and quiet whisper; "save me".

Shanley Hotel back in its day

Imagine what the stories this hotel could tell, after all it was built in 1845 by Thomas Ritch and had many owners over its existence. The Shanley Hotel is a 3 story Dutch Colonial Hotel, with a huge wrap-around front porch. Many of the previous owners catered to the wealthy. I will not go into the history of the hotel just yet, as I want to guide you just the way it was for me on my first visit.

Let me explain and I hope that I have not repeated myself, as I know along the way writing this I certainly will from time to time. I have followed just as I did long ago when I decided to visit the Shanley a philosophy to not research a location or get insight to a location, whether a private case or an event location where I may hold events until after I had visited the location and gotten my own "knowing" of the spirits residing. In the beginning it became sort of a way to kind of validate for me what was happening with my abilities and such. I still follow this practice more so as it is more validating for the clients and event guests than the need to prove myself to any longer.

So, here we go! The ride to Napanock was exciting. Colleen and I were both like two kids going on an adventure. We both were intrigued and scared. What were we getting ourselves into? Colleen herself was feeling much of the same feelings as myself. She had always known she was intuitive and truly was a history buff, with her family involved in genealogy. Her father was the president of our local Historical Society.

The Shanley was quite a drive. We spent our 4-hour drive, filled with conversations of all kinds. The drive itself was beautiful, as Napanock sits in the Hudson Valley of NY. It was full of rolling fields, small quaint towns and many older style stone houses with incredible detail and craftsmanship. It was interesting to see many of these old homes along the way, each representing their time period. In many ways it was a little like driving back in time a bit.

Napanock itself was exceedingly small, the Main Street you could easily drive right through it and wonder if you were there yet. As we turned onto the Main Street, there it stood right there; a huge sight to see. Like I said this massive 3 story white building, that kind of looked a little like a larger version of the Amityville house. It had the same arched roof. So, as we pulled into the parking lot, you could see all the work being done to the hotel. The porch and first floor were freshly painted and had this vibrant red door with a beautiful stained-glass window; "Spirits Reside". How cool was that to walk up and see this. The outside of the 2nd and 3rd floor was deteriorating and broken windows with plastic coverings.

What an overwhelming impressionable building just standing there. The back of the building looked like it was going to cave in with windows and doors that looked like they went to no-where. It was obvious this was a building that had many additions and changes throughout the years and to some degree was bandaged while sitting abandoned.

As we entered, both Sal and his wife; Cindy greeted us with such warmth and excitement. You could feel their love of the hotel and excitement of welcoming their guests.

Walking into the hotel I must tell you, was like walking into a heated attic. That is the only way I can describe it to you. It is that feeling when you are walking from a cooler room and going up into an attic that has a wall of dense air that hits you. This was what it felt like, but not the temperature so to speak, but the denseness of the air.

Big Great Room

I immediately felt like, wow my head feels a bit like it is going to explode and the beginning of a dull headache started. We got settled in our room which was on the second floor. As you came into the hotel the entryway was small, and the stairs directly in front of you. The doorway to the main large living room was to the left. Cindy showed us our room, which was at the far right of the second floor and at the end of this dark mahogany stenciled hallway. Every room, wall, floor and crevice of this hotel was stenciled. Or at least the first 2 floors. The hallway was beautiful, with statues of angels and gargoyles and old antique furniture. Each room has its own decor which was intriguing because you could tell how much love and work was put into this hotel.

Our room was beautiful! It was all in white lace, full of feminine charm with a small white cosmetic sitting table lining one of the walls. As I walked into the room, I can recall feeling the presence of a woman in the room and could completely imagine her sitting there in the vanity, brushing her hair. The room opened to a small quaint seasonal porch, with another bed and several bookshelves lining the far wall. It was also a beautiful room which had its own lure about it. This room made me want to just sit and write. I felt the feeling that someone had to have done that very thing. It felt warm and inviting.

We met with Sal downstairs in the great room, which he said was the common area. That is where he would always be for anyone who needed him during the evening investigations. We were not the only guests that evening that there were other guests that would be a part of the evening. The great room was full of sitting chairs and tables so you could make yourself at home. They had a coffee station which Sal informed us was going to be on all evening. Refreshments and water also were provided, and we were all welcome to bring our own food to store in the refrigerators if we would like. Sal basically said to make ourselves at home; the Hotel was always open as he considered every person who came here, his friend. He did not just say this either, he truly meant it and you could feel that about him.

We sat with him for a few hours it felt, while he talked about how he came to own the hotel. When Sal purchased the hotel, as I had indicated previously, he was planning on renovating it and bringing it back to a full functioning hotel to then put on the market. He explained that being in the construction field that he along with his friends and family had all the tools and experience to bring it back to life. He explained that there was no known evidence that the building was haunted. It all began to unravel a bit when they began to work on the hotel and during the construction of things began to happen. Many things such as tools being misplaced, hearing people talking but they were the only ones in the room. They had so many things happen that they began to lose track of what was what. Lights being seen in the building when the electricity was not even installed yet. Smells of cooking, perfume and often a strong smell of cigar lingered in the air from time to time. Imagine going to the bathroom and seeing a shadow in the mirror pass by! That scared the hell out of them and happened often in the downstairs bathroom once they were able to use it. Of course, they heard walking on the floors above them and the most chilling sounds of a woman crying on the third floor.

Sal explained how this was an occurrence for them all, not just he and Cindy, but anyone that was working on the renovations of the hotel. He said he recalled he and Cindy, who also considered herself sensitive but not something that was fully embraced at the time, and certainly not her focus when restoring the hotel. She and Sal remember sitting one night realizing that their hotel was seriously haunted, and they needed to understand by who and why? As they restored the building, Cindy also stated that most of all the decorating was done by the spirits. That is right! As the two became more comfortable with their guests, there seemed to be a common respect that was happening. Sal and Cindy stated that they felt very welcomed by the spirits and they felt the spirits that resided at the Shanley, were happy with their passion to restore the dilapidated hotel. Wouldn't you if it was yours? So here was this couple that came in with no intentions of it being a haunted hotel to feeling that they were going to have to head in that direction as who would want to stay at a hotel that was haunted?

At first the reality of this was a bit unsettling. No one was going to buy a huge hotel, fully restored to its beautiful 1800 décor, that was loaded with spirits and it was loaded with spirits. Cindy began to really open up her abilities and said that the hotel was just alive with more spirits than living people could ever fill it. They talked to her and she could hear them. As she sat in a room trying to decide what paint to put on the walls, she said this voice would come to her and a knowing of what colors, what stencils and designed to be created to transform that room back in time, just as the spirit wanted. When you visit the hotel, you will see that each room is uniquely different. This will explain why. Just like the Winchester House spoke to Sarah Winchester and told her to build and build, the Shanley spirits spoke to Cindy telling her what they wanted the hotel's décor to look like. I do have to say that is such a beautiful thing.

Marguerite's Room

As Sal and Cindy realized that the hotel was haunted, of course like anyone else they wanted to understand who was haunting the hotel and why? Sal explained that he and Cindy went down that road of discovery, learning about the paranormal and metaphysical tools to use along with inviting mediums, psychics and paranormal enthusiasts to come and check out the hotel. This then leads to expanding this information with research, as we all know so well, when research and documentation of "said experiences", is validated well that becomes more solid proof than anything. It is a great balance to have insight to a location and experiences, but when research can validate that experience, well magic happens.

Cindy explained that we would begin the evening with a small tour of the hotel, and she would bring the overnight guests around and fill them in the hotel's history, along with some of the claims and experiences. People could partake in this or choose not to. After the tour you were then on our own to explore the hotel.

As we sat there listening to Sal and Cindy informing us of the evening's plan, I could not help myself but be drawn to the doorway at the fair end of the room, which then entered into another area of the hotel; known as the Gentleman's quarters and Bordello. Obviously, not current but named after the previous establishment of the hotel. There was this feeling that a man was watching us, standing in the doorway. I could feel the energy of him standing there, watching closely. It was a very creepy feeling and I kept glancing over to that area and finally I recall, Sal noticing me. "That is the Guardian. He stands guard at the doorway. We believe he is the guardsman of the Gentleman's quarters and Bordello area, where back in the day when Mr. Shanley owned the hotel, he kept watch of all that was entering the hotel and no one passed through this area without his consent. I remember the feeling like okay, that was a bit validating but also running through my mind the reality that the longer I was in this hotel, the more aware of my surroundings I was becoming.

Colleen and I had plenty of time to unwind while we waited for the evening tour. We had hung out with Sal for a few hours and decided to head back up to our room to change. I recall, walking down the hall and feeling the energy of people all over. As we walked down the hall to our room, I could feel the heaviness in my chest, like OMG, I feel like I am going to have a heart attack. "Colleen, do you feel that?" I asked her multiple times and she completely was feeling the same thing. I felt this pressure like an elephant was sitting on my chest along with the dull headache. As I opened the door to our room, there she was sitting in the corner of the room. She was beautifully dressed in a white dress with lace and soft flowing fabric. Her hair was nicely coiffed on top of her head. A very elegant looking young woman. She had an elegance about her that I cannot fully describe and a combination of happiness and sadness all in her expressions. She stood there and looked at me with a small smile on her face. I froze and just looked at her. Omg here, we go I thought. Oh shit, am I seeing this woman for real? I entered the room and began to unpack and set my stuff out on the dresser, again, drawn to the adjoining room. I walked out to the room and there stood a man in front of the bookshelf. He was very faint and did not turn around, but I knew he was there. I came back in the room and sat at the vanity. Imagine the feeling of sitting quietly looking at yourself in the mirror of a vanity and having the sensation of a person touching your hair, softly stroking your head? Imagine looking into the mirror and feeling this while visibly seeing no one. This is what happened to both Colleen and I that evening in our room. It was quite the experience.

Time to head to the tour and off we were to have our "adventure", which by now, I was beginning to feel that my abilities were going to be front and center as they say. And they were!

Cindy first sort of did an intro into the basic information of the hotel. It is true beginnings before she and Sal purchased the hotel.

The original hotel was established in 1845 by Thomas Ritch. The hotel started its long history of being a very appealing place to stay for wealthy guests traveling from New York and Boston. The location, although remote and to many of us a bit out in the middle of no-where, for those in the city, this was a great retreat. A destination location for travelers looking to escape the city and enjoy fine dining and grand décor.

The hotel continued to have its fair change of ownership over the years. Mr. Hungerford purchased the hotel roughly 6 years later and the name became obviously the Hungerford Hotel and continued to cater to the high-class clientele and along with the gentleman's quarters and private bordello.

Beatrice Shanley and brother in law
John Faughnan who ran the hotel after
Mr. Shanley's death

Possibly Mr. James Shanley and associate John
Powers

Adolph Wagner bought the hotel in 1887 of which during his time, the hotel suffered a fire, burning the hotel to the ground. The hotel was rebuilt in 1895 and continued being the destination hotel of upstate NY.

On October 1st, 1906, the hotel was sold to James Shanley, who was truly a successful entrepreneur and saw a lot of potential in the hotel. He was a very well-liked man with personality and a bit of a true cutthroat business mentality. He opened a barber shop, bowling alley and a billiard room, along with the gentleman's quarters and bordello, he wanted to add many opportunities for all his guests to enjoy.

James Shanley married Beatrice Rowley and the two ran the hotel quite well. The hotel became the social hot spot with many glorious parties, activities, social high teas luncheons for the ladies and entertainment for all.

Many of the elite stayed at the Shanley Hotel enjoying the hotel as well as becoming good friends with Mr. and Mrs. Shanley. Thomas Edison and Eleanor Roosevelt were frequent guests and close friends. The Shanley's attended the Presidential Ball in Washington for President Franklin D. Roosevelt and Mrs. Eleanor Roosevelt made a great many appearances with Mr. Shanley.

Mr. Al Hazen (Owner of Shanley)

The Shanley Hotel

The hotel truly was a happening place in its day. Kind of funny how for different reasons this hotel still is a happening place, however, not for high tea luncheons or the activities of the wealthy men and woman that visited its halls, but for the paranormal enthusiast, who have had so many experiences staying at this hotel, it has kept its name alive and thriving.

Cindy did not want to tell us everything that had occurred at the hotel, but more of a brief introduction to its history adding some of the main tragic deaths that had happened at the hotel.

The hotel had its fair share of wonderful times and business booming. There were many documents and such about the bootlegging happenings of Mr. Shanley along with the story of him during the time of Prohibition, the hotel had a speakeasy for the benefit of its guests and the town's citizens. Many enjoyed the benefits of this secret room until the arrest of Mr. Shanley along with his partner, John Powers, who were arraigned in Federal Court.

I could write a book just on all the owners, stories and history of this hotel which seems so rich in story. But to save a lot of needless reading,

I will enclose some history as I go along and focus more on my own experience with the spirits here.

As Cindy bought us around, I remember feeling the pressure in my head of a slow headache that seemed to never go away. I am not one for headaches and this was quite annoying. I would soon learn that this is often a beginning sense of feeling spirit activity in a location and many who attend events with me also understand this feeling. It begins with a dull headache and dis-appears when you leave the location. I felt uneasy and nauseous most of the time I was in the hotel.

The entire time I was walking around during the tour I could just sense that this hotel was loaded with spirits. I was not seeing them just yet but could totally feel their presence. The crazy thing also was that it was not just one or two areas of the hotel, it was all over in every bathroom, bedroom, hallway and even a few closets from time to time. It has this feeling about it, like the hotel itself was watching you. I remember going into the bathroom at the end of the hallway of the second floor and having the total knowing that there was a lady laying in a pool of blood in the bathtub. I was not seeing her directly but just this knowing that something happened in here. It was the most uneasy feeling being in that bathroom.

When Cindy led us up to the second floor where most of the finished rooms were, I remember standing in the doorway of what was known as "Marguerite's room", a room rich in mahogany colors. There were around 12 that were staying at the hotel that night and everyone had gathered in the room. No one was wandering around in the hotel. Sal was downstairs in the large gathering room. I had my back to the hallway and was trying to pay attention to what Cindy was talking about, but honestly I don't think I heard hardly anything of her tour as I was totally distracted by the hotel's spirits.

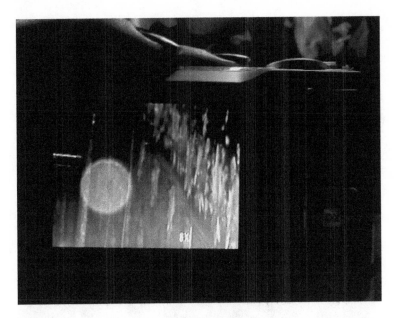

Spirit Orb in Hallway

As I stood in the doorway, I could hear someone beginning to walk down the hallway towards me. I did not want to move and could feel the presence in the hallway. I had my camera in my hand and slowly turned to face the hallway, taking several pictures of the entire hallway. I could feel the presence walk past me and down the hall. As I looked at my pictures, there was clearly a large bluish orb in all my pictures, the orbs appearing in different locations down the hall. Okay, here we go! Man, this is going to be an interesting evening I thought to myself.

I could go on about many of the experiences like this in the hotel that night, but what truly this story is about is the one that stood out as my most profound experience that really propelled me into my mediumship abilities.

Colleen and I had your typical haunted experiences at the hotel that night. We heard voices, captured EVP's in the basement that were as clear as someone talking out loud in the room. I listen and share this EVP often on my Facebook, as it is just undeniably a spirit answering us. Clear as clear can be. We had seen large orbs appear out of nowhere and heard sounds and doors open on their own. For us both, one of the most startling was when we had gone to bed which was the bedroom at the end of that hallway on the second floor, known as "Esther's room". My favorite room to this day.

We both slept in the queen bed and there was not much room between us. We each had our back to each other and were just randomly talking a bit about our night, when we both started to feel the sensation like someone was in the room. We simultaneously felt the presence of someone get on the bed and lay down between the two of us. I remember being a bit like, what the hell is this? OMG!! There was no denying someone laid down between us and we both were frozen in a little bit of fear. We did not sleep very well that night.

Spirit Orb in Bordello

Early in the evening, we went into a small room in the bordello. The bordello was incredibly intriguing. First, you had to walk through the doorway that I had felt the presence of a man staring at us during our meet up with Sal. As you made your way into the small hallway, there was a door on the right that led to the bordello rooms. The stairs were narrow and dark. As you made your way up the winding stairs, it opened to a small sitting area with 3 adjoining rooms that you could easily see right before you. Each room just had a nice decorative curtain as a door. I felt such a strange variety of emotions in this area from excitement to sadness.

I cannot even begin to tell you the strange emotions that hit me in this area. I felt as I walked up the stairs which, like I said were very narrow and tight, it was like ducking into a dark area that you just had no idea what was going to meet you at the end of your destination. I had the clear image of an elderly woman sitting on the little bench tucked in the corner of the bend of the stairs. She reminded me of the woman on the movie Beetlejuice, who was tiny and smoked cigarette after cigarette. I just had this feeling she was watching us as we passed by. As I got to the top, standing in the center small sitting area, it just felt like this was not a "happy" place as many led us to believe during the tour. Cindy and Sal had stated that the spirits of the Shanley were there because they wanted to be here still and yes, I felt a certain level of comradery with the energy of the hotel, and later during multiple visits I would totally understand the reasons for this feeling and agree, but this visit, I didn't feel like this area was happy. There was an excitement feeling for sure but not totally sure why or by who.

Colleen and I settled into the center sitting area for our first attempt of communicating with the spirits in this area. Colleen sat on the small day bed that was posing as a sitting area on the far wall. I sat in the rocking chair that was across from her. I had my notebook and pencil in hand as I wanted to also write anything I was feeling and as I said wanted to document our full experiences here. I remember so clearly feeling this presence coming up the staircase which was behind me. I told Colleen to take a picture of me as someone was coming up the stairs. When she did, a huge, large ball of light, which we learned later that it was a spirit orb. It was as clear as could be hovering above my head. It had its own light, which is what made it distinctive, because we were sitting in the dark and there was no flash when the photo was taken.

We felt the need to go into one of the small rooms which was known as Maddie's room. As I sat on the bed, we pulled out our dowsing rods and began to ask questions. We were totally engulfed in asking if this was a woman or male and a whole series of questions.

When using dowsing rods, it is best to know that it still is a mystery how these things work, but they do. They follow the same physics of using a pendulum, which will sway back and forth for a no answer to a question and sway in a circle for a yes response. It is quite fascinating how these devices work, but they do, and they are great tools for communication. Over the many years we have used other devices, such as flashlights to help in communications, which also 2 flashlights can be used to represent a yes and a no. Spirits amazingly can turn on individual flashlights to answer your questions. Honestly, when you have a good connection with a spirit, they will try extremely hard to use anything to let you know they are there and talk to you. I had an experience during a private gallery that the spirit used a small tabletop lamp to turn on and off for us. The spirit was the son of one of the guests attending which was so incredibly emotional for us all. It was quite the experience.

Colleen and myself used the dowsing rod quite a bit as we both wanted to ask questions and again at this time, I was not embracing my abilities, so I was relying on this cool tool.

As I sat in that room, I began to get emotional and uncomfortable. I was feeling a totally overwhelming feeling of sadness and began to sob. I felt this woman was not happy here and she was lonely and sad. She was not as everyone was describing as being happy to be here at the hotel and the spirits are always in and was taking on a different meaning with me. I was beginning to feel remorse and that this was not right. Why was this woman here and why was she making me just sob? I looked at Colleen who was feeling all these emotions also and we both just felt like this was not a happy place for this woman. I remember looking at

Colleen a few times, like omg, why am I feeling all this? Colleen was such a great person to have accompany me, as she did not make fun of me or tell me it was nothing, she was quite supportive and knew that I was experiencing a deep connection. Colleen herself had abilities growing up but never fully explored, like myself and she was having many of her own moments of feeling the presence of spirits throughout the entire hotel.

Like I said I could write a whole book just on all the different spirits and experiences at the Shanley Hotel over the years, but this one I really want to focus on my experience with who I would find out was called; Marguerite.

This is where my awakening and embracing began...

After a great stay at the Shanley, I took all my notes and experiences and gave Sal a big hug goodbye. I was going to be in touch with him over the next week as I wanted him to read my article and guide me with any questions that I may have. I also talked to him about returning possibly alone for a weekend extended stay. He was more than accommodating and really was so easy to chat with.

We headed home on a Sunday afternoon, tired and exhausted. As I said goodbye to the hotel, little did I know that I never did say goodbye to the hotel.

Monday morning, I was getting Nicole and Garrett off to school and felt like I was in such a fog. I still had the dull headache and nausea feeling from the hotel and felt like I was still at the hotel. I felt sick to my stomach and drained. I knew that I had little sleep the entire time I was there, but this felt different. I had no idea that this was one of the "sensory six senses" that many felt when around spirits. Now it is like second nature to identify and understand that signal, but back then, I was like what the hell is wrong with me?

Seriously, I was not sure if I needed to go back to bed or make myself throw up and be done with it. It was such an eerie feeling to me, but I felt like the hotel was with me. I felt like someone was watching me and came home with me. But how is this possible? Don't they just stay there?

So, I decided that since no one was home and had the day to myself, that I would pull out my pendulum and see if anyone was with me. I sat in my bedroom and began to ask; "Is there anyone with me?" "Yes". "Are you from the Shanley?" "Yes". "Are you a woman?" "Yes". I continued to ask questions and quickly knew that there were 2 females that came home with me. Great, now what do I do?

I wanted to understand why they followed me and just who they were. I was so excited to hear that one of them was Esther. She was clear that she was curious about me and where I lived. She had said my property reminded her of places she visited, and she loved the stonewalls. I had such a great feeling of warmth and love from this woman. She had this gentle feeling about her, like the mom that you could just sit down, and she would comfort you best she could. As I used the pendulum, there was something odd happening to me. I noticed that I could sort of hear the answers in my head and almost knew what to ask and many of my questions sort of shocked me that I knew what to ask. They were not typical questions, they were more conversational questions, just like the topic of what she liked about my property. I sort of knew what she was feeling and wanting to say to me before I asked out loud. I felt that she was with this other woman, and although Esther was happy and seemed to come and go, this other woman was not happy.

The hotel had information on Esther, after all she was an important person at the hotel. Sal had told us that her presence was strongly felt by many people.

Beatrice Shanley had a lovely sister named, Esther Faughnan, who lived with her husband, John in what was known as the apartment area on the second floor. This was the area that Colleen and I stayed the weekend we were at the hotel.

Esther was described as a very lovely woman who enjoyed her time at the Shanley and enjoyed entertaining the guests. There is a bit of debate as to the passing of Esther, but we do know that she died young and left her children to be raised by Beatrice, who had lost several children in childbirth. The story goes that Esther died in childbirth; however, I have not researched the history to find out for certain.

So here is this woman visiting me at my home. She was clear that she would be returning to the hotel but wanted to see where I lived. I thanked her for coming and truthfully was touched and honored. I felt like, wow this is crazy that this is possible, but why not I suppose, as we get in our cars and travel where we want to go. So, it only makes sense that spirits travel wherever they wish to go.

I then asked Esther if there was another woman with her and she said, "Yes". As I began to tune into the other woman, I immediately got that feeling again of loneliness and despair. I could feel this woman and asked her if she was the woman that was making me cry in the Bordello area of which she answered, "Yes". It took me some time to figure out who this woman was and began to ask her to spell her name. I would ask the Pendulum if her name started with an A and continue down through the alphabet. It was long and tedious, but I wanted to know her name. She spelled the name Marguerite.

What was going to transpire truly was to this day as I type this, crazy and insightful for me. I still look back and think, how the heck did this come to be all from a simple visit to this hotel to write an article. But it changed my life.

Marguerite wanted to talk to me and share her anguish. I truly felt this woman needed to have a friend and someone to listen to her, and I just happen to be the one she felt comfortable to talk to. At first this was with use of my pendulum; asking her questions and trying to get a grasp of who she was and why she was at the hotel and above all, what happened to her. You see, the Shanley Hotel did not have any information on Marguerite. The only insight they had of the existence of this woman was a room on the second floor that they named; "Marguerite's room". It was named because many guests who have slept in that room have been woken up hearing a man yelling this woman's name. That was all they had.

So, I continued to ask her questions the best I could. I had a full day of trying to grasp these two ladies visiting me and then also needed to pick up my kids and cook dinner and tend to my life. I was totally unaware that Marguerite had no intention of leaving and never wanted to go back to the hotel.

So, my journey began with Marguerite being around me for the better part of 4 months and I am not kidding you. I woke up the next day and continually had this feeling of her being there. I had intense headaches which I never get. I tried to take Tylenol, but it did not work. I felt so sick when she was around, but I also wanted to honor her by listening to her, as I felt this woman is in pain and needs help. After a few days, I called my mentor of many years, Janice Tarver. Janice is a medium that my mom had seen many years ago. I had gone to see her with my mom and over the years saw her now and again. I can remember so many times Janice saying to me that I had abilities, but I never really thought about. There were times that when I made an appointment to see her, it was more to ask her lots of questions and truthfully, just make sure that some of what was in my head was real. She could always tell when I needed to touch base, as she would look at me and say, "you need a reality check, so to speak." Janice also taught me the healing modality of Reiki and another empowering course called Avatar that I to this day teach and use many of the practices in my life coach services.

I reached out to Janice to make sure I was not literally going nuts. I called her up and said, Janice, I do not want a reading, but can you tell me who is around me. Janice tuned into Marguerite immediately, telling me that there was a woman with me, and she needed my help. She explained that this woman felt a bond with me and that I needed to not shoo her away. Okay I thought but what am I supposed to do? I have no idea how to help her or what to do. And by now I was really feeling this woman's anguish and it was making me sick. Janice told me to talk to her like a friend, be her friend and tell her to back away from me when she was making me sick, but to follow through and give her Reiki and listen to her as she needs someone to listen to her. Okay, so

I am not imagining this and there really is a woman with me. OMG! she is real. Not that I doubted spirits at all, as my god, I was the child growing up who saw and heard them, but I had not been down this road in a long time and this is happening and it's real!

So, each day I would talk to Marguerite and listen to her. She became an extra guest in my home and not only myself could sense her, but Nicole and Garrett both felt her in our home. As time had gone on, I had to explain to my family that this woman had come home with me from the Shanley Hotel and I was trying to figure out how to deal with it. I do not recall totally telling my husband, Steve at the time, as he was not fully excited about the paranormal or spiritual experiences that I had. He I believe thought I was slightly crazy, but he loved me for it. I told my kids who were more intrigued and obviously feeling for themselves that something was going on in our home. We began to have lights flicker and at times see movement here and there. Nicole came home one day from school and said, "Mom, Marguerite was in school with me today. She was pretty matter of fact over it. Garrett also said he felt her come up the stairs and stand in his room from time to time. He was not scared as he knew that I was trying to help her.

As I began to log down all my conversation with Marguerite there were times, I was honestly thinking I am losing my mind. I can remember the day sitting in my sunroom and just put the pendulum down and listened to her. I could hear her talking to me. A woman's voice talking to me in my head and knowing it was not my voice. I then saw her standing in my sunroom. A beautiful woman with long red hair and greenish looking eyes. She stood before me as clear as could be. She had this angelic look about her but was so quick and sudden that as soon as I began to register the seeing of her, she was gone from my vision, but I was still able to hear her. I thought, holy shit, I am losing it. I am going to be put away in a nuthouse. How am I going to tell my husband that this woman is here, and I am seeing and talking to her. When I finally did tell him, he was casual about it and I think tried to process his own belief systems and thoughts about this all. He did believe me though and knew that Nicole and Garrett were vocal that she was real.

I remember the day my mom came out to visit for a weekend and was sitting in the living room. Suddenly, she jumped up from the couch and told me a spirit woman just walked across the front yard. She was totally in shock. I had to clue my mom in about what was going on and surprisingly she didn't poo-poo it, because she saw it and she also said that visiting me that weekend she had a headache the entire time. Okay, so we all were having headaches and it was so frustrating and painful. I began to request much needed breaks from Marguerite. When she was so close to me that I felt I was going to throw up, or my head was going to burst, I would simply ask her to back away from me a bit and explained to her what her energy did to me. I asked her to just give me some space from time to time and she respected it. I am not sure where she went but truly do not think she went back to the hotel. I like to think maybe she went to other areas of my house and as I type this, I think that is one thing that I should have asked her. But she did give me breaks. There were times I would have to take a few weeks off having her around. That was how intense her energy was.

My relationship with Marguerite became like a kindred spirit. We were connected and I felt every emotion she shared. She was truly a gift to me in so many ways and I value the time she spent with me. I am teary as I type this. Someday maybe she will visit again and say hello, but I truly feel she is at peace and some place that she is deserving to be.

So the process started with me writing down all that I could process from her and this was something that I guess I have to explain mediumship a bit to those who may be reading this and wonder how this all works. You see, I had no idea there was a difference between being a medium, psychic and just having intuitive abilities. I really was not trained or educated, but more so learned as I went along. The whole process at times stills baffles me and wish that someone could truly explain in a scientific simple stupid explanation of how this is all even possible. Deep within me, I know but my brain and intellect just sort of get in the way. What is in my "knowing and heart", battles the "brain" and what we are taught to know and believe.

Marguerite began to tell me that she traveled by train to NY. She was a young girl seemingly in her early teens, wanting to escape her life at home and go on an adventure. She had wanted to make something of her life and had this thirst for adventure and her own life. She had come to the Shanley Hotel to find work any way that she could and thought this would be the greatest place. By now the Shanley had a name for itself and was the destination place for those in the city wanting to venture out for summer vacation and social gatherings. Mr. James Shanley's hotel was the place to go. A grand hotel settled in the deep woods of Napanock, NY.

She was young and began to work helping tend to the hotel's needs, often what we would refer to as the general housekeeping chores of the hotel. That was how she described it to me. She was hired to help clean, serve and assist the owners and guests.

Somewhere along the line and forgive me for we could never really validate any of this information fully. This is often the case with cases that are dated back in time periods where records are not always documented and so hard to find. I will share with you what Marguerite told me and shared with me about her life and death. This is my own version and by no means can I prove or say 100% prove this information. The fact that Marguerite existed at the Shanley I can validate, and I will get to that shortly.

So here she is, seemingly enjoying her arrival at the Shanley Hotel. She expressed that she was so excited and happy to be there, as the hotel promised so much and for a young girl who seemed to be fleeing her old life, or possibly seeking adventure, this I did not know. I just knew that she got on a train and headed to the hills of NY in search of a new life.

She continued to explain that her time at the hotel started out as she had imagined and helped the owners with the daily tasks of running a hotel. At some point things changed and this I am not fully sure the timeline of when it did and what the circumstances were. What I do know is that the hotel had on one hand, like I had said earlier, a grand time of socialites and gatherings during the time period of many of the owners. However, there were also the, let us just say, the "secret" shadier parts of the hotel. There seemed to be a time that the bordello, and activities of the bordello and gentleman's quarters was a normal, possibly welcomed profession and business. After all the time period of bootlegging and gambling had its mystery and desire and really wasn't looked down upon, but this seemed like for Marguerite she was forced into the bordello activities. It pained me to hear that she was forced to partake in "all" the guests desires and requests and not just housekeeping. So, for a young woman who sought adventure, found herself dependent on the hotel's owners for her livelihood, but that paid a price.

I was not sure fully the timeline of when Marguerite was at the hotel. I could not tell if she was there during the time the Shanley's owned the hotel but did know that she was there during the time that Mr. Al Hazen owned the hotel. This was when things got difficult for the young lady.

Marguerite told me that she had been raped multiple times by the owner of the hotel and that he had sort of taken her as his "play toy". He was not a nice gentleman and would yell for her when he wanted her. This was not an easy thing for her to share with me and believe me during this whole time I was just overwhelmed with lots of emotions and empathy for her. I could feel her sincere sadness and honesty for the physical life she lived and regretted to some degree. She was mourning her life even in spirit and that broke my heart.

I was trying to understand why this woman came to me and was here in the now. This whole experience was quite a revelation for me on many levels. First, like I said as a kid this was an ability that I had but never in my wildest dreams would I talk to the spirits that I had visited. Second, what does this all mean? Don't we just move on after we die? Why do we linger? What really is the reason that places are haunted? All these things were going through my mind, while also wondering if I was losing my mind. A spirit is talking to me and telling me her life story. I have got to be losing it!

Marguerite was by nature a gentle woman, she was very kind in how she talked to me and I felt a true friendship evolving between the two of us, as I was honest with her that this was all new to me and I would help her best I could, but I may be a little out of my league with what to do. I genuinely believe she just wanted someone to listen to her and know her story. After all, everyone that came to the hotel had no idea who she was. She was a spirit that lurked in the shadows, maybe a presence you feel but cannot quite see or get to answer your questions with the paranormal devices that people use. Maybe many have felt her anguish and did not know which spirit that these emotions were coming from. This is totally possible, and I have learned this time and time again, as I do this work. It is kind of like being in a crowded room when you go to locations that have multiple spirits residing. Imagine saying hello to a room full of people, well, more than one will respond back and if you are trying to talk and get a line of communication going and asking many questions, well, you may have several trying to answer. Therefore, it is so important to really try to establish one on one direct communication so that you are really listening to that spirit which is reaching out to you. This is how it was with Marguerite. I can only imagine that night I was at the Shanley, she knew I was "feeling" her and quite possibly she already knew something more about me than I knew that night. The fact that I would listen to her and ultimately help her spirit move on.

Marguerite talked about the night that she fell in love. She was miserable at the hotel and dealt with the trauma of the owner having his aggression and affection taken out on her. The owner she described was not a loving kind man and drank until he was a monster, often abusing and raping her repeatedly. She totally felt trapped. She was forced to tend to male clients along with the other woman and this seemed not the same way the days of woman enjoying working in a bordello and selling themselves for sex. I do think that there was a time that this was not looked down upon and women had their own sexuality and desire to please themselves and please customers for a monetary value. I think of the time of Burlesque dancers and the art of sex and dance as being quite a beautiful thing along with the time period of women having some power over men in a world that they did not. Hard to say fully because we did not live back in those times and we can only imagine and gather our beliefs based on what we were educated on. Either way, I did feel that on one hand there were women who may have enjoyed their time working in the bordello. I was shown that there was this time that this owner had more of what appeared at least in how Marguerite expressed to me, a sex trafficking sort of vibe. I was seeing images of women being lined up in the back of the hotel and hosed down and cleaned in large bathing sort of procedures, which for me was quite frightening to see. Marguerite would show me in vision much of what she experienced in her life. Along with listening to her telepathically and at times using my dowsing rods when I needed to double check what I was hearing was correct. I also saw quick flashes of scenes, just like going through a slide show to better help me see what I was hearing. It was quite difficult to live my daily life while she was with me. And Marguerite was with me for the better part of 4 to 6 months. Now that I am writing this, I realize that she was with me for more like 7 months because she traveled with me to my mother's that year for Thanksgiving, who lived at that time in Pennsylvania. Wow, all this time I have been saying that she was with me for 4 months and that is not the case. It is so hard to believe!!

It was hard, like I said to live my daily life with all this in my head, so to speak. Between the images and empathy toward this woman and trying to not just break down and the headaches and awful feeling my body encountered when she was with me, I just can't believe at times that this all was even possible let alone a reality.

Marguerite fell in love with a customer that came to the hotel and although I am not sure exactly how this relationship began and evolved, I know that she was elated to have a love and someone that was going to take her away from the hotel. From what I gathered this man saw in her the young woman who truly wasn't meant to be here to just service men. I say this with no dis-respect to the other ladies that worked in the bordello of the hotel, but for Marguerite, I believe this man fell in love with her and promised her a world beyond the Shanley hotel.

Marguerite was in love with this man and her joy was growing again with hope. She told me that he was coming to save her, and she anticipated his arrival one fateful evening. That evening turned her whole world upside down again. Her hope and joy were taken from her just as quickly as that day she endured the lifestyle she was forced to participate in.

Marguerite's love never arrived to the Shanley nor did he ever return. It broke her heart and she fell into deep sadness. Where did he go? Why did he not come to get her? I can only imagine this was devastating for her.

I am not fully sure of the events that transpired after this, as I said this was never able to be researched properly due to the time period along with little information to fully go on. I would call Sal, the current owner of the hotel and update him of this woman. Sal himself was also trying to research her and find any information about her that he could. He too was having a hard time validating who she was, although he believed me and knew that many guests previously heard a man calling out to this woman's name, but that was all he knew.

Marguerite suffered her fate one night when the owner of the hotel took her life in a fit of rage. From what she shared with me, he was upset that she was leaving, and he would not allow any man to have her. He viewed her as his property, and no one would have her love but him. From what I could feel and see, he had strangled her and stabbed her taking her life and discarding her body in an unmarked grave. No one would know who Marguerite was. Her life just discarded like a ragdoll that you throw away after the newness has rubbed off.

I cried half that day and thought, how the hell am I going to help this woman and how am I going to get through this myself? I was becoming very rundown and drained with all her emotions and sadness on top of my own feelings for what this woman endured. It was heartbreaking and thus began my questioning of why she is still there and why has she not moved on to the "heaven" everyone talks of? Why would she stay at this hotel that brought her nothing but pain and sorrow? I just did not understand this, and my mind was running in circles with a million questions of the afterlife and ghosts and spirits.

I began to ask Marguerite many of these questions and learned that she was truly "waiting" at the hotel for her love to return to get her. He was not able to come and get her in her physical life, so she waited for him in her spiritual life. What a tragic love story this was.

Marguerite understood that she was passed. She tried to explain to me where her body was buried but it was so hard to not only get this information but fully hear her with that much detail. I am not from NY, nor did I have any idea where she was talking about. I tried to explain this to Sal as well, and it was really a dead end to ever try to honor her grave with a marker or such. I also had a lot of questions of where her family was and did, they ever try to find her? Chances are that this was the case, but how could we possibly know. I never got Marguerite's last name. I look back now and know all the things that I would have done differently, well not necessarily differently, but more all the information that I could have gathered from her so that maybe I could have been able to fully validate her life as she so deserved. I was trying to understand and grasp this whole experience without losing my mind. I also could not just drop my whole life and take off to NY to do all the work it would take to find these answers. These communications that I was having with her were in between my daily life of taking care of my family.

She was trapped in this feeling of remorse of her life, regret of her choices to go to the hotel and feeling such a loss of not knowing why the man she loved never came back to take her away from this all. She was choosing to stay at the hotel and hide in the shadows in hopes that his spirit would come look for her.

As Marguerite shared all this with me, I truly felt I had a better understanding of her life and the need for her to sort of make peace with it. I talked to her with compassion and empathy, just as if she were my best friend and I was trying to help her get through it. In many ways Marguerite was my best friend at this time because I also talked to her about this whole experience and how I felt about life and death and what happened to her. I allowed myself to cry for her and feel all her emotions, which strengthened our bond.

There was a day that I remember what Janice had said to me about allowing her to grieve with me and then provide her healing so that she could move on and make peace with herself. I remember sitting under my tree in my backyard and talking to the invisible person sitting next to me and thinking, okay this is really a road Karen that you are going down and now you are committed, so you can't have this woman with me forever, you are going to have to help her see that she can't return to the Shanley but she also can't stay with me forever. There must be more for her in the spirit world. This is when I began to counsel Marguerite, much like how a therapist may listen to their client and then at some point when you have assessed the situation, you approach the time that it is best to provide the tools to help that person move on in their life. Time to help her.

Marguerite was very thankful for me listening to her and she wanted to have her story known, which is what I promised her I would do, but she also wanted to have help in healing and forgiveness. I began to talk to her about the reality that we are spiritual beings, and this was a life she lived, and yes, she was totally wronged and deserved so much more. How would she have known that getting on a train to head to NY would end up with this outcome? She could damn herself forever, but she was young and had no one to really help her, so in many ways she needed to forgive those choices and be gentle herself. How can any of us ever see the road ahead? We cannot and we go along in life making choices and alter our path along the way with the resources we have at the time. I talked to her about how she was choosing to stay at the hotel but just maybe there was more for her if she left. I asked her if she saw the area that she may be able to leave if she wanted to. She answered me yes, as many have also answered me yes when I have asked this question.

Spirits seem to be able to see the area, much like a road possibly that is ahead, and they know they can go down that road, but they are afraid to. So, they stay in the familiar area. I also know that Esther had been a big help with comfort for Marguerite's spiritual life at the hotel. It seems that she took her under her wing possibly in spirit life and was there for her, but that too left me with questions. Why is Esther there?

She seemed happy though and liked being at the hotel and seemed like she was able to come and go. Why has she not helped Marguerite fully leave? I had so many questions that needed answers. As I write this now, I realize that this was the beginning of my journey into the world of the paranormal and spirituality. As you read all my stories, I will share all the insights and wisdom that I have learned all these years, but for now, this was just the beginning of those ponderings.

The day under the tree I began to do some Reiki for Marguerite. Reiki is an old form of energy healing and has provided many people benefits. I wanted to help heal her and provide some peace. Each time we did this, I could feel her energy becoming freer to me. I felt between talking to her and helping her see that she had more to her existence than the Marguerite that lived at the Shanley and the Reiki session, helped her see. I feel she was seeing that she was not going to find the love of her life or her family if she stayed there and that she needed to see beyond the Shanley and look at what was out there for her. She needed to make peace and forgive herself for what happened to her and then make the choice to move on.

The day this happened I will never forget. I sat under the tree again one day, it was a quiet peaceful day. You know the kind of day that you sit outside, and the air is perfect, the sounds are relaxing, and the world just seems good. This was that kind of day. I sat with her and opened myself up to her energy and truly didn't know what I was doing but just opened myself up for her and opened up to the higher energies that exist and surrendered to the universe. There were vibrant colors and swirling bright flares that I can only describe as being in a vortex of bright lights and dashing images of color and warmth all around me. It is something to this day I cannot ever explain because I truly do not know how I do this but also how to describe the experience. It is indescribable on so many levels. All I know is that the amount of love and peace that I felt at that moment was utterly amazing and as quickly as this was happening, it was gone. Marguerite walked into that swirl of color brightness and faded away.

I remember the feeling after sitting in my yard, under the tree with such the strangest feeling. A stillness that was left. Feeling like I was just there and what the hell just happened combined with okay, what just happened? Where did she go? Who did that? What did I just experience? Jesus, Karen, who the hell are you going to tell? But it all felt good. It felt amazingly, normal, like I have always had this ability within me, and it was no big deal. I sat there for some time, alone with my thoughts and really wondering if this woman would find her true destiny and thanked her for sharing this all with me. I was hoping she knew that she forever changed me.

For a few days I felt lonely and lost a bit, after all this woman had consumed my life during her stay with me. It was hard to really grasp all that had occurred and to be honest, it felt very much like I was living a dream. When was I going to wake up from this experience?

After a few weeks passed, I woke to that familiar feeling in my room. I could feel the clamminess happen again and slowly opened my eyes to see a man standing in the corner of my room, near my closet. He was dressed in a dark woven suit looking jacket and pants, from what I could see. He had a very old-style looking hat on, of which he tipped his hat to me, almost like an introduction or hello, nice to meet you. At first, I was startled, as I always am with my night visitors, but his eyes were sweet, and his expression was gratitude. It took just a moment for me to hear him speak and share with me that he was Marguerite's love. He was the man she was waiting for and after a few moments of telepathy conversation, he informed me that he had been trying to reach her in the afterlife, but she was unable to see him. He explained that he was returning to the hotel to get her and met his death by 2 men. This man was beaten and then hung somewhere on the property of the hotel and disposed of for no one to find. His soul has not rested knowing that Marguerite would be forever wondering why he did not return for her. He had no idea the fate she endured and that she was forever waiting for him to return. As the man began to fade away, I had this comfort within me. I could see the silhouette of her dress and figure standing with him and then her beautiful smile as they faded away.

Two beautiful souls waiting for their love to be reunited! I cannot tell you how this felt for me as it still to this day brings tears to my eyes. How can this be? How can they not find each other in the afterlife, I asked myself time and time again? So many questions still unanswered and possibly I will never know.

I don't recall the timeline of the day that Marguerite came back to me but it was shortly after the man came to me, and then it may have been a few months as time was really hard to keep track of during this whole experience. I was going about my day and cleaning when I felt her energy come in. I was so excited to see her and feel her presence. Her words were forever etched in my heart! "Thank you." She smiled at me and thanked me. I began to sob something so fierce within me, as I had never felt this kind of joy before. I can only explain it as the moment you give birth to your child and your whole body is overcome with incredible joy that just can't be contained. That is what it felt like. I just broke down and sobbed for her happiness.

How can I possibly explain this experience in words? I try the best I can and do hope that you feel it as you read this. There were so many things for me.

During this whole process, as I stated that Sal was trying to also validate for me the identity of this woman but we both could not find researchable information about her existence at the hotel, until one day when Sal called me out of the blue. He had come across a woman in town who not only remembered the hotel during its grand time, but she could validate seeing the beautiful Marguerite, whom she described as a beautiful red headed young lady with hazel eyes that often sat on the front porch. She had believed her name to be Marguerite. When Sal told me this, I was beside myself. I had never doubted my experience with this woman, but to have this validation was priceless to me. She existed! She was there!

My experience with Marguerite profoundly changed me! I began to realize that my abilities were given to me for a purpose. It was not just about the curiosity of spirits and ghosts, UFO's and strange happenings in our world, it was about life and death and our spirit, our existence!

Sal

So, my quest began to not only understand my abilities and to not be afraid of them any longer, but to fully embrace them and be an assistance to spirits that are lingering in locations. There is far more to the story of the lights that go on and off in a building, or the object that moves with unseen hands, or the sounds of voices and names echoing in the walls. There is the spirit of a person, who lived and loved. There is a person who had family, had joy, sorrow, regret, accomplishments and guilt, all emotions that everyone human being has in their lifetime. There is a reason why some go very quickly and possibly peacefully to the other side and then there are those, like Marguerite, who have a story that keeps them held back.

A tragic love story in the physical world, finding eternal love in the spirit world...

The Lonely Man

Private Residence
Gilsum, N.H

In a small New England town lies the story of another tragic love story. A home that resides in the center of a small quaint and secluded New England town. I was called here by a client to help her understand the paranormal activity occurring in her apartment. Her two young boys continually woken each night by an unseen visitor. The boys would run into their parent's room, crying and scared and yelling; "There is a man at the foot of my bed, and he tickles my feet", the one youngest boy stated.

Imagine being a small child seeing a man in your room at night, not only looking at you but also touching you? I can totally understand this fear and concern for both the boys and their mother. I remember this fear all too well as a child growing up seeing people in my room.

Children often are very receptive to seeing spirits and feeling the energy of the unseen. They still have their innocence and creative imagination, which is such a wonderful attribute. Children are so receptive as they have not been conformed to believe what is told to them but allow information and their surroundings to truly be pure and real.

Children are extremely sensitive in many ways and are truly living authentically with their emotions, feelings, insights both visual, audio and sensory sensations fully open to receive. Many children are fully aware, but not all, and many will outgrow these abilities. There are also many, like me that these abilities you do not outgrow, and they stay with you permanently.

I have had many cases with children who have seen and were aware of spirits and imaginary friends to slowly lose that insight as they grow.

Often parents are not sure how to handle when their child fears their room, with ghosts and seemingly, goblins that are going to hurt them. You will laugh at me, but as a child I can recall being a bit afraid of my room also. Laying there in my bed at night and having all these things happening to me, with no explanation as to why. I recall one night laying in my bed and hearing things, swearing that Bigfoot was outside my window and thinking okay, well if he really is there, then I better talk loudly about how great and awesome he is so that he won't want to hurt me. Seriously, don't laugh because that was what was running through my mind. No wonder my parents had no idea what to do with me. Imagine hearing your child in her room, talking out loud to no-one and talking to unseen things?

So many kids have this feeling of being scared. I can totally relate to my clients concerns. What was so interesting with this case was that my client also was feeling many things in the apartment as well. She saw some of the spirits that were possibly there and she herself was learning a bit about her own mediumship and intuitive abilities. She had taken a few of my workshops and attended a gallery before reaching out to me. She knew that I did not want to know anything about the experiences, so she didn't tell me what she was seeing, but she did feel that she needed to know who was there and exactly what was going on to better help herself but also her two small boys.

The ride to her home was quite beautiful and I often find myself in new towns and places that I have never been. Gilsum NH was quite a ride that day, with twisty roads. I did not mind as it was on a hot spring day and I found it quite relaxing. I had asked for no one to be home, as I usually do, that way I can totally be alone in the home and fully tune in.

I pulled up to this 2-story yellow house, with a small yard. It sat just a few streets from the main street of town. It had a feel about it for sure and as soon as I walked in the front door, I could feel the energy in the home.

The main entrance of the home led into an open hallway, with a large winding staircase to the left of the entrance and my client's apartment door straight ahead. I was totally drawn to the upstairs and felt that the upstairs was "calling" me. It was an odd feeling as I stood at the foot of the stairs, observing the marker of crosses and religious quotes on each step leading to the upstairs. There were religious quotes on the walls as well. My immediate feeling was okay, what am I getting myself into? The upstairs tenants obviously have some concerns, either that or they were deeply religious, and these were reminders of faith. I did not have permission to wander up the stairs and wanted to honor my time at my client's home, so I just noted to myself the stairs and continued to her apartment entrance.

As I walked into her apartment, I entered the living room with most of the rooms in her apartment visible from the living room. I immediately met a man's presence standing in the doorway of what looked like her bedroom. He seemed to be an older man, with some robustness to him. I was not sure if it was weight that he had one or just a robust personality, but that was the feeling I had from him. His face was round, with either little or no hair at all. He had the feeling of being a little grumpy but also seemed to have a soft side to him. He was a strong energy there. I could feel a few different men in the apartment and often when there are multiple energies in a location, it can be a bit of seeing, hearing and feeling the emotions of many at the same time. I often describe this as being in a room with many different people trying to talk to you at the same time. It can be hard to differentiate upon the first immediate tuning in. I often feel like many are trying to get my attention at the same time and I must sort of direct my attention to one at a time.

What is interesting about mediumship abilities is that they come from so many different directions. They come from spirit but in many ways, such as feelings, images, sound, smells and impressions that are left in the location along with just plain knowing and often trying to sort it all out can be simple and quite difficult all in the same time. I love locations that I go to and one spirit is there and all my insights I know are coming from this spirit, while others may have multiple and that is when the challenge begins.

So, it felt like I was seeing one man and another man was talking to me. There was a man talking to me about living there in the home with his wife. He was overly concerned and talking about his wife. I stood in the center of the living room and was very drawn to the window that faced the street. I saw a spirit woman standing in front of the store that was in the town and visible from the house. I had this feeling she was looking right at me and the house and knew there was some tie to the store for some reason and could see her sort of pacing in front of the store. I also felt that the feelings of a townsman and like a funeral home was some place nearby, thinking of the houses close by had to have some tie to a funeral home of some sort. I would focus on listening to the man and then kept being drawn to the store and heard him make some reference to the store and that he and his wife owned the store and felt like some sort of tie to the town and possibly other property. The woman kept looking up behind the store a bit and just stood there looking at me, which was kind of odd because my thoughts were why is she there and he is here? Is that his wife he is so concerned about or someone else?

This man was very tied to the house and he knew he scared the people living there, and he was sort of saying that it was funny for him. Almost in a way that he found it fun that they noticed him and that brought him joy, even though it was scaring them. He referred that he was choosing to stay there and that he did not always think he was a nice man. I just took all this in from him best I could on my first visit.

Out of the corner of my eye, glancing to my right, looking into the kitchen area, I could see the shadow of another man standing in the doorway that was leading to what I would assume is the back yard. He was just glaring at me the entire time I was in the apartment. He was on the sort of skinny side and disheveled looking, with a thin face and long beard. He had piercing looking eyes and stood there with what appeared to be some sort of ax.

I felt he had a shadiness to him, and he just stared at me but did not say anything to me right away. Many thoughts were coming to mind as I stood there taking in his energy along with the energy of the home.

I wondered if he was related to the other man, and why is he carrying some sort of axe? Did he do something?

At one point I had gone outside to look at the property which had a small brook that ran along the driveway and around the back of the house and out to what was now a highway off through the woods. I had this weird feeling to go to the back of the house and look in the brook. It felt to me like there was blood in the water. Why? I have no idea, but it was like something was showing me this. The whole property felt like it was the oldest house in the neighborhood to me, like this house had meaning in the town and some of the surrounding homes didn't exist and some clearly felt they had a tie to the house as well.

I often will talk out loud to the unseen spirits and let them know who I am and why I am there. I know I don't need to do that because they seem to already know, like that whole telepathic communication takes on a whole other meaning, when they seem to just know I am there to listen to them personally and be of assistance. I often wonder if that is why in all the locations that I have been, there is always a feeling of welcoming, even with the ones that have truly not had such a pleasant disposition.

The man began to open up and told me that he was related to the man but didn't really say how or who he was. I felt he had some sort of tie to the house and the family that lived there. He was also saying there was an injury in the home, and he felt he may be responsible for it. Of course, my initial thought was "Oh, great, so he has an axe. What did he do?" He stayed in the kitchen area and I felt he was a presence that seems to be coming and going and did something outside. I wasn't sure if the axe was for cutting wood or what exactly it was, as it didn't look like a normal axe to me. He quickly just left, like okay that was all I was getting from him today.

As I continued walking around, I felt a small boy running upstairs. He would come to the top of the stairs and peer down with a curiosity towards me. He never came into the apartment and just came and went.

I began to talk out loud to the gentleman that was the main presence and told him that I was there to help understand why he was still lingering and who he was. I was truthful with him that he was scaring the family and that was not okay at all. I explained my purpose there and told him that I would appreciate it if he would stop scaring the children by standing in their room staring at them and I would be coming back to listen to him and be helpful.

I am always truthful with the spirits that are strong in my client's home, regardless of the reasons why they are there, they need to know that I will be their "therapist" best that I can and that I am there for them with no judgement but that I am also there for my client. I am there to work with them both but if they continue to be an issue for my client then I will have no problem helping ensure they "banished" from the property.

I know that sounds harsh, coming from someone who wants to help spirits that are lost move on and find peace, but a few things you need to understand about spirits. Living in a haunted home is not healthy for the living. Often time and time again, a person who lives among the spirits will have health issues and their quality of life is strained. It is one thing to have spirits that come and go and check in with a home or business they have great fondness of, or to possibly be lingering a bit, and then those who have a strong presence because there are several factors that they do not feel they can leave or are afraid to leave.

Many religious belief systems of heaven and hell truly can play into this feeling of just what makes a person, good or bad and where they are going to go. As stated before, our beliefs have a lot to do with how we live our lives and the choices we make, living and in spirit. Some of the craziest cases I have worked with priests that are afraid to move on because of things they did while living. Let that sink in a bit. If you ever wondered about religion, think about that for a moment. If the priest does not honestly believe that his sins are abolished and forgiven in his death, then that says something as to the validity of what they preach while living. The truth be known, we do not know 100% the afterlife until we are there. We know 100% it exists, yes, but all the details are left for our imaginations.

While at the home, I could have sworn that I heard the name Paul but was not sure who said that to me. So, I made a mental note for Angie and, she would hear it in my voice recording while at the home, that there may be a Paul in the home.

I then decided to just turn on my EMF meter and walked into the children's room. As soon as I walked into the room, it was like walking into a heavy dense environment. I walked over to the closet area and held the meter up to the door, which it quickly flashed into the red numbers. What does that mean? Well EMF has been associated with spirit activity but also for environmental fluctuations that are already in the home due to electrical wiring and plumbing. Often, we may use that to get a sense of what areas of the house have natural environmental fluctuations and areas that have no reason to be shooting into the red area. Like flashlights, many spirits will also use the EMF reader to communicate with you. You can ask questions and ask the spirit to light up the meter. I personally do not use it a lot but for some reason this time I thought it may be interesting to see if it had any kind of reaction to the environment.

Being in this room, I totally got the feeling that the man had either been ill or died in this room. It is hard to explain. I can only explain it as the example of how many have used dogs for specific abilities to sniff out illness, blood and missing persons based on scent alone. Well, for me it is like this deep heavy intense and nauseating feeling, that is far stronger than just having a spirit being in the room. I knew that this room was an issue, and no wonder my client's boys are having a hard time in this room. Anyone that is sensitive will be affected, even if they do not see or hear spirits, they will feel the energy of the room.

This really gave me some idea of what was happening at this location. I was not sure exactly the full details but felt confident that I could send my client a basic rundown of my first visit and return to understand all specific reasons that her place has these spirits.

The Return

On my second visit, I was able to get a bit more insight. I always feel like I am coming to meet my friends. I was welcomed again by the "main" man of the house and I could see that he was not an elderly man. His energy was happy to see me and I could feel that he was happy that I was there. He has such concern for his wife and wanted to know where she was and told me that his family owned the store, although he also at one point made it sound like his wife's family had something to do with the store also or that general area of where the store was. He was so lonely and did not fully understand what happened to him. He seemed very confused about his death and needed to understand what happened to him.

Family ties, he indicated. He said there were a lot of family ties in the town and that he had pressure to succeed. He felt he was beginning his life and had a wife who he adored and a small child who he also adored and now they are gone, and he is confused. He told me that he was aware he was passed, as I often ask this of the spirits who seem confused, but he felt like he was ill and then things went blank for him. So, this was for sure a mystery to figure out for him and for myself. Just what had happened to this man and why is he still feeling he is needing to be here in this house?

As I continued to talk to him, it became evident that he was growing attached to my client who happened to be a young mother of 2 small boys and having some marital strains. A young couple just beginning the strain of not only being young, but having a family was pulling on his heart. Parenting is a lot of work and on top of working full time and sorting life's challenges, well, it can be a challenge for any married couple. This man felt he wanted to interact with my client and her boys, and he was not very fond of her husband. He was talking to me in a way that made me feel that he was sort of intertwining his wife and child with my client and her boys. My client and her small children were sort of taking the place of his wife and child. He was also in mourning of his own life and what happened to him, so these emotions and circumstances in my opinion are the beginnings of many red flags. Spirits that become "attached" emotionally to living people is never really a good thing.

I am often asked if possessions are real and if attachments really do happen. The one question or I should say, a statement that is often repeated is "I don't want a spirit to come home with me and attach to me". I can totally understand this concern. As I have stated earlier, yes, spirits will come and go and may follow you home. It is their own curiosity, just as you are curious about them, well, they may in fact be curious about you, however, in general the spirits at a location are not looking to hitch a ride with you. I will say, though that some do, and you do have to always be aware and careful. Possessions are not something that generally happen overnight. Most people do not go to a haunted location or move into a haunted house and become possessed by a residing spirit. A spirit that is looking to really attach to you, well they will wear you down over time and you may begin to notice your personality and traits changing if you have been living in a location with a very strong spirit that has this intent. But normally, this is not the case. There have been many situations where people who have sensitive abilities are living in a haunted home, feeling that they are being possessed by the spirit but in fact it is more that the spirit is trying desperately to get them to understand what happened to them. I have a case I will share later that truly was this situation and one that took me a great deal of time to get my client to understand what was happening to her. But that case will be for another day.

On my return visit, Angie came along with me. She had begun to do some of the research of the address and felt that she knew I would want to have some information sooner than later. Again, as soon as we walked into the house, we were greeted by the "men" of the house, I like to say. Kind of a funny terminology, but it was true.

What is cool with working with Angie is that she has her own abilities when doing her research. She has mediumship abilities that she has played with a bit but also will so kindly state that she is not a medium. She does not like to draw attention to herself and shares a similar story as a child living with parents who could not really understand or help her with her abilities, so for many years she did not embrace her talents.

When Angie does research, often she has the feeling of the spirits coming to visit her and sort of help guide her along the way to find all the necessary details. It can be quite fascinating when it happens. We may be struggling to find a certain detail and out of the clear blue she will call me with the missing piece. "How did you find it?" I will ask her, and she will chuckle and say well, "I had a little help".

So, on the second visit, Angie also was aware of what seemed to be 4 males. I thanked them for not scaring the children as I had touched base with my client, and she assured me that the house felt calm after I had left.

On this visit, it was clearer that there were 2 men that were related and some tie to the house. The first man that I felt was very much a strong presence in the home and was establishing an attachment to my client as he was truly loving the children in the home and my client being a young mother, he felt some sort of bond with her but was not related to her. This was the man that I felt extraordinarily strong in the boy's room, where I do believe he either died or was extremely ill in that room. He was afraid to leave, like he was waiting for something or someone, possibly the woman that still was showing herself in front of the store which was visible from the window of the house. He kept looking out the window towards the store and you could feel this sadness and longing.

The other strong male that we both were tuning into was in the large bedroom of our client's home. It felt that the bedroom was more of the main living room of the house in its day, as the home was now divided into a 2-family home, with one apartment downstairs and one upstairs. This man was immensely proud of the town and that he had a big part of its success and he traveled throughout the town in spirit and often visited other homes in town.

Angie also was aware of the other man that was in the kitchen area. She could smell the sweat as if he were a worker and said she felt like he was passing through and left as quickly as he came.

I was just still so drawn to why the woman was there looking at the house and obviously had some tie to the house and then here is this man in the house that is sad and longing for something or someone, confused and very depressed. He was confused about his death and afraid to leave the house. The man in the kitchen felt he had some guilt and was part of an accident. This man also seemed tied to the house in some way. So, this was a mystery to figure out.

Angie wanted to take a ride and show me the town and a few places that were calling to her and seemed to be validating a bit of what I was tuning in to. She wanted to show me some of the village maps of the town and some landmarks from modern time and some dating back 250 years ago. There were things of interest that were found in some of the research that she had done in a previous visit to the town.

High in the hill there stood a house, on the left side of the road, just past the store. The day she visited the town this home kept calling her, making her continually drive up past it and then ironically, she would end up turning around in its driveway. On the fourth drive by, she placed the car in park and folded her arms on the steering wheel and said, "Ok, what is this that you want me to see?" As she looked at the home and the layout of the yard, it was noted that the house was a simple rectangle double floor home, the windows were old and had the old glass wave to them. To the left of the house was a building resembling a shed. The home was calling to her and wanted her to notice it, but the question was why? She sat there for 10 minutes and just observed.

Old photo of the farm on the hill

There was a cemetery on the same side of the road as the house, just before the house on the right. There was still a lot of snow on the ground and not a clear place to park, but she noted this was a place to return for a visit.

The rectory for the congregational church that was on the main street was in the back over the first fire station across the road. Also, behind the store was a row of homes built on both sides of the street. The now post office was once a general store that sold all sorts of items and the rear section you can still see the footprint of where the building was attached to it.

Angie just wanted to show me these places as they called to her when she was researching the house and town. We never know what valuable information is or what is not when we investigate a private case, so when anything gets our attention or we have a feeling about, we make a note of it.

With each visit to a home, the spirits are now becoming more comfortable with me and will begin to share more. I always feel like they have assessed my purpose and possibly understand they can trust me.

At this point Angie wanted to clue me into the beginning research that she had started on the house, as she felt that it would only help me with validation. She knew who I was connecting with in the home. Once we can identify the spirit or spirits that I have been talking to, it is amazing how quickly a bond occurs. When you can address them by name and have them validate intricate details of their life and story, it just intensifies the whole experience. The unknown is now known.

This investigation was now becoming quite interesting and we had no idea just how emotional this case would be for us both.

Angie's Beginning search

In the 1838 map of Gilsum there is no evidence of a cart path, road or any other home in the Memorial Street area of current today, nor is there a listing for the surname of Newman on the map. Angie was projecting that this is one of the spirits I am talking to and the fact that this man truly made this town known.

The road that goes by the church and up route 10 does exist and there is a household of E. Jones on the end going up route 10. The next household going up route 10 from there is that of J. C Guillow; this appears to have been the beginning of Memorial Street. (There was no street that existed there at that time.)

The Cemetery that is past the present store on the left as you turn up to go to Gilsum center is on the map of 1838. The present post office was not there, where it is located today, and it appears to have been a pasture. There are two schools just past the cemetery. There is no indication of a church on the 1838 mapping.

Upon looking at the maps, D. Ware homestead on the left-hand side and next to the right is I. Loveland homestead. (Isaac Loveland is Esther's Loveland's Father. She married George W. Newman.)

1849 George W. Newman built a house and resided in it until 1863. (It is believed this location is outside of the town of Gilsum as per the map not listing G. W. Newman on a map til 1863; appearing to head to Alstead via now route 10)

1863 George W. Newman purchased the David Ware House built in 1838, which was the Old David house built in 1800. This house was just past the cemetery on the left past the present store and just after the schoolhouses that sits on the right. The next house on the right is his father-in-law Isaac Loveland's home.

1877 Map of Gilsum- This map does not show above the current cemetery and road that cuts off to the right all the way to the end. It does, however, show what is now Memorial Street and the G. W. Newman store with the house attached, also shown is the Blacksmith Shop that G. W. Newman built for his son; Charles Dudley Newman to do Blacksmithing and Carriage making. Also shown on the map is the Congregational Church.

So as all this is being documented it is apparent that Mr. Charles Dudley Newman was the man I was speaking with. This is my client's home, and his father was George W. Newman who clearly established the town.

1877 George W. Newman built this house (my clients house), for his son C. Dudley Newman. Charles Dudley Newman has occupied it to the present time listed in the town of Gilsum, N.H from 1752-1879. Dudley had learned the trade of Blacksmithing and carried on the business of carriage making a year or two. He raised fowl, rabbits and smaller pets. Paul Langlois lived in the house with Mr. Newman. This was known as the Newman's Wheelwright and Blacksmith's shop. The Blacksmith's Shop is pretty much how it was built in 1877.

1892 Map of Gilsum-Again they have cut off the upper part of Gilsum on their mapping, above the cemetery. Angie felt George Washington Newman was still residing at the Old David Ware/David Bill Farm, Alstead Hill Road. G.W. Newman has a home at High Street. G. W. M. Co located at Main and High Street. G. W. M. Co. on Rte. 10 Gilsum Road. G. W. Newman is located at Main and Memorial for the Store/ Post Office and the Blacksmith Shop and another house down 4th from Main Street and 3rd from Rt. 10 to Main Street. G.W.M.B. Co. There are two buildings, speculating that these were the Tannery's.

So, in fact Mr. George W. Newman had a great deal of ownership of the town and truly was a part of making it an extraordinarily successful growing town. It totally made sense to me that he was the stronger presence in the living room area of the home and sort of came and went as he had many places in town to visit.

There is a great deal of information on the Newman family tree, however, the most important information that we will share is really focused on who these spirits are that are "haunting" my client's home. It is extremely hard at times to not get totally lost in all the details of a family's entire lineage as it is quite fascinating. I could write half this book on each location and its entire history. I try when investigating to find the necessary information that really pertains to the spirits in the home; their identity, the bond or attachment of the property and how to be of assistance so they can find peace, closure and move on in their spiritual development. That is my purpose.

Newman family

On our third visit we had more correspondence and could really get to the heart of the issues at hand and the family ties with the house. George W. Newman was born in 1818 and married Esther Loveland.

George W. Newman was born in Keene and grew up in an industry with good management. He had acquired a large property and built more houses in Gilsum than any other man. He was engaged in the manufacture of lumber, in buildings and in framing. He served as town selectman and justice of the peace. He built the store and house on the corner of Sullivan, and his sons carried on the business until 1878.

They had 7 children. Florentine died at little over a month old and Abba Stella died a little over 4 years old. Fay died at age 23 of Insanity. I wondered if this could possibly be the young boy that was running around the house upstairs? I wondered this only because of the cause of death being insanity but we were never able to connect with this young child.

Charles Dudley Newman was born November 15th, 1857; married Jennie Louise Carpenter Nov 15th, in 1877. He died on October 23rd, 1887 at the age of 29 of Typhoid Fever. His daughter, also named Jennie, was 1 year and 9 months old when he died.

Charles Dudley Newman had his property described as the Newman Sawmill, all real estate-Sawmill & Tannery situated in Gilsum. He was a very well-known man and promising of upcoming greatness in the town to follow in his father's footsteps. This was the other man in my clients' home. It totally made sense to me that he was young and died from an illness and was bedridden in the home not too long after he was diagnosed with the "fever".

What a total tragedy for this man, who was seemingly, on his way to having a successful business, beautiful wife of 10 years and a new baby daughter. My heart just felt so sad for him and now I understood why he was tied to the home. His father built this home for him and he would carry on the family name, probably with many children of his own and an ever-growing business.

The one name that came up during my first initial visit was the name; Paul and I remember saying in my audio recording to Angie that I was not sure, but one of the men's names may be Paul. I am often so hesitant to say names, even in readings as once you say a name you hear, and it isn't the right one, well, all your credible information seems to go out the door. It is funny how many people do not understand that being a medium is not like a direct telephone line with clear audio to the spirit. Yes, sometimes I can hear things clearly, but other times I cannot. As stated earlier, often there are many spirits around so when you ask for a name out loud, well others can answer who have nothing to do with the house or the group. So, when I hear a name noticeably clear being said then I will just say it and then see what happens. I love when a spirit however will spell their name with the dowsing rods and it really is them. It is a Yippee!! moment.

In 1877 Paul Langolis lived with Charles Dudley Newman and helped with the Blacksmithing business. This seemed to be the man with the funny looking ax standing in the kitchen. I was not sure yet his story, but we will get to that later.

The other gentleman in the home that I first described as having not much hair and tickling the kid's toes was a grandparent to the boys. My client validated this after I had told her my first initial meetings. So, this was truly a touching moment that she knew at least one of the spirits her sons were seeing was their grandfather and that brought her great joy and relief.

On the third investigation we really got the opportunity to dig in and talk more candid with the spirits. I was overly excited to address them by name and understand far more from them personally.

We decided to go to the house and talked to Charles who preferred to be called Dudley. So, I addressed him this way moving forward. He was welcoming but really wanted me to find out what happened to his wife. He wanted to know where his wife was and was not as talkative on this visit. It was like he was more confused and withdrawn about his death and why he was there and where was his wife. So, our investigation took a turn. I needed to connect with the woman, but how am I going to do this because she will not come to the house. I had this knowing that she was not going to come to the home.

We got in our car and drove by the store. Angie had felt the woman may have been trying to connect with her when she had first visited the town. She may have been a part of her driving up past the store where this spirit woman's father had originally lived. Angie and I drove around that day to all the Cemeteries and did not fully begin to connect with Jennie until we got to the Woodland Cemetery. When I saw her standing in front of the store, she was this beautiful young woman dressed in an old dress and her hair neatly coiled on top of her head. She was always staring at me and pacing in front of the store.

Angie had a real twist to this story. Jennie Newman was not buried next to her husband Charles Dudley Newman in his family plot in Gilsum. This would instead take us on a ride to Keene, NH to the Woodlawn Cemetery. Angie and I were standing at a section of a family plot. We cleaned off some of the moss on the large gemstone and found it interesting that it was the name Bowker. According to the research, Junie (Dudley and Jennie's daughter), after her mother had passed away 30-40 years and I found interesting and funny that she still wanted this to be her mother's first married name in all her documentation to be known, instead of putting her mother's maiden name, she made sure to put it in the Newman's name.

So, I am asking Angie if this Bowker is her second husband? She says no he is not buried here, and she did not know where he was buried. As I asked her this that familiar feeling came over me and then there, she was standing right next to me. Jennie was here and her daughter Junie was with her. I felt such excitement that she was here and that she has reached out to us. I could feel them standing there just listening to us talking and could feel a bit of hesitation and emotion coming from both the women.

I ask Angie if it is correct that these two are the only two of the Newman family that are buried here, and she tells me this is correct. The Bowker headstone was put here. Junie had married a Mr. William Coughlin. They purchased this plot from Holmes and the Proctors; Mr. Proctor is on the other side and the town has this as one whole lot.

Okay, so who is Mr. Proctor? And how is Jennie and Junie connected to this family. This was becoming very confusing to me. Why is this woman not buried with Dudley? Is this why he is wondering where she is? This was becoming like a jigsaw puzzle with lots of missing pieces.

Angie chuckles and says, I have no idea how they are connected. She thinks that maybe Dr. Proctor took care of Jennie medically. There was no indication that she worked for him, so maybe with her being diagnosed with Asthma from childbirth this was the family doctor. It made me think of how my stepfather, who is also a doctor often took care of some of his elderly patients who had little money or family.

I found it incredibly sad that this woman was married to Dudley for 10 years and was not recognized in the Newman graves, and that she was not buried with her husband. Her husband was buried in the Gilsum Cemetery, and here she is buried not even with family.

So as the story goes, Jennie married her second husband after Dudley had died. She had married Fredrick Bowker in Gilsum. Bowker is not buried in the Woodlawn Cemetery and neither is Junie's husband Mr. Coughlin. Jennie Newman was only married a short time to Fredrick Bowker. Mr. Bowker was married previously and divorced due to severe cruelty. He passed away of heart disease after just 10 years of marriage. This was just about the same time frame that she was married to Dudley Newman. After Mr. Bowker passes away, Jennie and Junie move to Keene, N.H and the two women live alone at 135 Elm Street, Keene, NH until Junie marries at the age of 33, Mr. Coughlin. Mr. Coughlin was quite a bit older than Junie and was a wealthy man. His business was in meat production and ran a Cheshire Meat and Produce company in Keene, N.H. He also died before Junie. Ironically, George E. Newman, involved in real estate and carriages and sleighs business and lived on 3 Central Square and lived at 103 Lincoln, who was Dudley's brother and uncle to Junie. Jennie and Junie moved from 135 Elm Street to 67 Winchester in 1920 and Mr. Coughlin moved in after Junie married him.

There was the question whether this house was purchased by George Newman for the two women? Was there sympathy from the Newman brother? A woman who was not taken care of by the Newman family. Then Mr. Coughlin passes away and there is no documentation of him being buried in the Cemetery either. When Jennie passed away did, they bury her in the Woodland Cemetery to maybe have her closer to her daughter, Junie so she could visit her grave as often as she wanted? This was beginning to be an incredibly sad tragic story for sure. It is sad to think now Junie is left by herself with no family, no husband and no children of her own and where was her grave? We could not find her gravestone. She was buried in the Holmes and Proctor plot with her mother but no marker for herself.

The Holmes and Proctor family in some way relate to these two women. A connection that obviously was strong enough to bury them in their family plot. Maybe they became friends and felt bad for the women and took care of them. There was obviously no one to take care of them at the end of their days. Normally, if you are not buried with your husband's family you would be buried with your own parents, however Jennie Carpenter's parents are not buried in this Cemetery either.

What was awful was that when Dudley passed away, his father did not take care of his lovely wife and child. His father still owned everything they had and although they set aside personal items for her, she was asked to leave the home. The house would go back to Mr. Newman along with all their possessions.

So, in essence she stayed in the home for what looked like four years and then moved on. I was beginning to feel that Jennie wanted to now start talking to me. I could feel my emotions beginning to build and I wanted to just hug this unseen woman. Both Angie and I were feeling a bit overwhelmed with all the reality of this woman's life story.

So, I began to open myself up and listen to her. She was totally acknowledging everything we were talking about. She proceeded to tell me that Mr. Newman didn't have much value for her after her husband died. He was quite cruel and harsh. He made her feel and was open to expressing to her that it was time for her to go find herself another husband to take care of her. The men in the family built the business and wealth and it went to them. Jennie Newman did not choose to leave the house and was mourning her husband. Her feeling of her husband abandoning her was echoing in my ears and feeling overwhelmed with a new child and no one to really take care of her properly. Her family did take her back in, which was located just past the store, but she did not stay there awfully long it appeared.

She told me she was happy in her home with her daughter and that was her safe place. That was when she felt alive and at peace. She visits that home often, she said, and she comes to the store to look upon Dudley, but she will not go in that home. It was heartbreaking for her and a part of her was angry at him for what all transpired during her time with the family and dealing with his death. Honestly, I could hear her say that when she moved to her new home, she was free. She felt free.

Jennie was young when she married Dudley. She did love him and was a faithful and dutiful wife, however, she did not choose to marry him. This was an arrangement that her father and Mr. George W. Newman made. She was to be the producer of children, cook, clean and be a good wife. Dudley was a good husband and a genuinely nice man, who adored her and took care of her aside from the family demands of his father with business. She explained that her second husband was out of necessity and she had not the means and Mr. Bowker was truly kind to her and her daughter.

I explained to her the situation with Dudley and how attached he was to the current residents of the home and explained to her that he does not understand what happened to him. His illness was confusing, and he almost seemed like he was waiting for her. She did tell me that he does not see her when she stands at the house looking at him. She can see him, but he seems to not see her. She had concern for him also and does not want him to be stuck in that home either. It was incredibly touching. She went on to explain that she had tried to go to the house a few times and Mr. Newman would not let her. This is in spirit, this man still having dominant control over the house and his son's affairs.

When I probed this further, it appeared that Mr. Newman blames Jennie for Dudley's death. He believes that she poisoned him. He believed that she poisoned him with bad food. It had something to do with a lunch that they did not all have the same thing and something special and she did not make the food, but she insisted that a lunch be packed. He was going to the mill that day to work.

I did ask her if the man Paul had anything to do with the illness and she did say, yes, he knew about the contamination. So, what did that fully mean? Was their knowledge of contamination in the food or water they were eating at the mill? Why the statement that she wanted to pack him a lunch. This was a bit confusing. I did ask her if Paul would have any reason to harm Dudley and she stated "No" he did not.

I was now aware of her daughter Junie and she felt like she was a heavier set woman who was a bit of a handful. She was incredibly happy with her husband and said he was a good man. Junie felt she wished she knew her father because he was a good man from what she was told, and she wanted her mother to be acknowledged. She felt so heartbroken that he died so young and what her mother had to endure. The mother and daughter bond were very touching and throughout this whole communication, both Angie and I were often in tears.

Jennie did explain that Dudley had gotten sick with a fever and it took over his whole body, leaving him bed ridden. He had been in and out of consciousness and died about a month after he was ill. It took over his body very quickly. They confined him to the bedroom with no visitors. She and her daughter were not allowed to see him. Both Angie and I wanted to go back to the house and talk to Dudley and fill him in on all that we had discovered and that we found her and his daughter. The tricky part would be getting this family reunited. To have Dudley feel he could let go of the house and open himself up to "see" Jennie and Junie and understand on a deep level that they did go on and live long lives. This goes back to the validation remarkably similar to Marguerite's story of not being able to see beyond their own existence. To not be able to see beyond their grief and sorrow. All this time, Dudley is staying in the home, mourning the loss of his own life, the loss of his beautiful wife and daughter and not seeing anything else for himself.

The other true tragedy was also that their daughter, Junie did not have a head stone. Where was her headstone or any reference to her? Not only was Jennie Newman discarded by the Newman family, but so was her daughter, the first granddaughter in the family. Where was the grandmother and other woman in that family to override Mr. George Newman? How could a young woman grow up and live a full life without any of her own bloodline recognizing her with a headstone in the end? This was possibly one of the other reasons that things were unsettled.

So, one beautiful crisp spring day, Angie had picked me up with her trunk full of supplies. She had a shovel, blanket and a small headstone that she had made. It read; Jennie Grace Newman Coughlin 7 October 1866 to 1 December 1970 "Junie"

Angie at the Cemetery

The Stone Angie had made

We dug the hole and placed the stone for all to see. It was touching and one of the reasons I love working with Angie, as her compassion and true integrity of the purpose of all the work we do speaks for itself. We will forever be grateful for this moment and the two of us felt like we have done a beautiful thing for these women. Our day was not done, as we gathered ourselves and took a moment to breathe in the air, dry our tears and head down the road back to Gilsum to go see Dudley and share with him the story he needed to know. Just heartbreaking thinking of it all!

Whether this family would be soulmates in the afterlife, I do not know. That is one that I have learned is not always assumed. Just because people are in each other's lives on earth does not mean that they are soulmates. We each have connections and yes some are powerful and the thought that we all will be best friends and family in the afterlife, is one that I can't give you a solid answer on.

I did, however, feel that Dudley needed the closure of seeing his wife and daughter for him to be at peace and both Jennie and Junie understood. The only concern that they had was whether he would come out of the house to meet them and that Mr. Newman would also allow this. I was amazingly comfortable letting her know that she didn't have to worry about Mr. Newman, as I will make sure he does.

When we returned to the house, I had no idea what was going to transpire but we both felt that we were on the right path and had a bit of a plan. Ironically, it was Paul that greeted us first. He started talking to me immediately and felt he was there when Mr. George Newman died, when he had his accident and he tried to save him. He kept showing up with blood on his hands and the accident was with a tree. I did not know if they were working together cutting the tree down, but he said it fell on George, but he felt very responsible for not being there to help him.

Then I remembered that when I first arrived, I had seen blood in the water. So, it made me wonder if he either washed his hand in the brook or did it happen near water?

I felt Paul sitting next to me and the feeling of remorse and worry was coming from him. It felt like he needed to get this off his chest. I asked him more about it. I asked him if he had cut the tree down and he went on to explain that they were clearing an area and Mr. Newman came to check things out as he was involved in everything and often made rounds to all his businesses. The piece he said was up on the hill and now there was a house there, but they were clearing the land and Mr. Newman came to check on them. I asked him if he and Mr. Newman had made peace, if he had seen him and he said he didn't know. He comes to check on him, but he does not see him. He just wanted him to know that it was an accident. I talked candid with him and told him how at first when I arrived that he had startled me a bit standing in the kitchen with what looked like an ax and I couldn't help but wonder what he did. I explained to him that he will have the opportunity to tell Mr. Newman how he feels, and we can hope that it will give him closure. I knew that Paul was not completely staying at the home and was not Earthbound as I say. I truly felt that it was just Dudley that was more Earthbound.

Mr. George W. Newman was 75 years old when he died in 1892. He was killed by a fallen tree and buried in Gilsum. So, this explained the situation and concern of Paul.

I went into my client's boys' room and waited for Dudley to come talk to me. He came in just as I had expected. I could also feel Mr. George Newman was in the house and observed and I told him that I needed to talk to Dudley and to please be patient. I could tell he wanted to talk also.

Dudley came in and sat on the bed with his hands on his face. He looked like such a young man, feeling like he was being scolded or something as he began to cry and had this nervousness about him. He does not know what to do and he paces the room often. He went on to tell me that the man of the house, meaning my client's husband does not treat her well and he doesn't know what to do. I understood what he was saying and told him I sympathized with him and they were a new married couple with 2 small boys which can be extremely hard on a new marriage. I told him how thoughtful that was that he was concerned for her wellbeing, but he also needed to understand that she was living her life now and he was in spirit and that it was not healthy for him to hold on to being here.

I explained to Dudley that Angie was going to fill him in on the details of his life and what happened to him. I explained to him that he had become terribly ill with a fever and was in bed extremely sick. His body began to shut down and he lost consciousness and died very quickly. I told him how at times when we have tragic deaths that our spirit is sort of confused as it is separated from our body in a tragic way and sometimes it can leave this void. I continued on to explain how he is sort of like a caged bird in the house and he can see the house and the rooms with the new family that has moved into the house, but that they are of the present time and not of his life. I expressed the joy that if I say opened the window, he would be able to fly a bit higher and maybe go see the tannery or the other homes and stores in town. Angie then continued to let him know that she had done all the research and found his wife and daughter. As Angie started to talk to him, I periodically asked him if he understood what we were telling him of which he nodded. I started to see him crying and it was the release, and I could feel it in him, like he was becoming clearer to really grasping what was being said to him.

Things began to come together and at this moment Mr. Newman came into the room and was listening with his heart as well. I could feel the whole energy of the room changing. I explained to Dudley that his wife, Jennie and his daughter Junie were standing outside. His daughter was showing herself as her younger self to not startle him. I told him if he looked out the window by the fence, that he would see them. Junie was a cute little girl with very wavy brown hair and was standing there next to her mother. She grew into a beautiful young woman who took care of your wife and they became a great mother and daughter team, a family with lots of love. Your wife missed you and loved you, It was hard for her when you passed as she had this wonderful husband and the two of you started your family with your beautiful daughter before you were taken from her. She was not honored after your death; your family did not honor her, and she saw all her future of the life you would have had together swiftly taken away. She is very much at peace now and she wants you to come sees her; your spirit is not meant to be in this house. I explained it was alright to come visit any time you wish. I explained that his father comes and goes and does not stay at this home.

At this point, Mr. Newman was understanding this all and wanted him to know this also. He stood next to the door and wanted him to know that he was sorry. It was hard to have this very stern and tough man begin to understand the hold he had on his son and he wanted him to know he was proud of him and that his life was taken too soon, which made him very bitter and angry. Mr. Newman wanted me to know that I was misunderstanding him, and he cared for his family. I understood and it was not for me to judge any of them, but to help them see deeper into themselves.

As I type this, I am teary as this is always so emotional for me to be a part of this process. This is part of my transcript of that moment.

"Dudley, I would love to know as we cannot see your world. Can you see? Do you see where there is light? Can you see where it is coming from? Can you see it around you?" ... "Yes, I can."

"Has the light always been there? See the light, see the spot that comes around it? "Yes."

"I've had people tell me that they know where it is. Can you see this house as if you were living in it back in your time?" ... "Yes."

"Dudley, what is past that door is your family, your mom, your dad, your daughter, your wife, your family and your friends. People that you knew and in such a beautiful way. You see the life that you knew as

Charles Dudley Newman is a small piece of who you are. It is only a small piece. Your spirit, your soul, everything about you is meant to go through that light, to go through that area, because your purpose is so much higher than being here. You need to trust Angie and myself and walking through that area could be the most beautiful thing that you could ever possibly have and that you could say goodbye to the pain that you have had from dying so young and being sick and going through what you have gone through, of losing your future of what you wanted to happen in your life and your vision of having a lot of children and having this house grand and running your father's business. All those things you can say goodbye to. Does this make sense to you; what I am saying?" .... "Yes."

"So, my question for you is this, I am going to play a beautiful song for you. It is a biblical song. It always seems to be a healing song. I don't know what's going on out there; beyond here. I can feel it and sense it by your father's peace, I think he comes to this house to mourn what happened to his son, because of what your father's eyes are saying to me. You had business sense, you were not cutthroat like him but you had a heart, the others, he was harsher on them. He was harder on them; he did not see them being able to handle everything with the business. He was worried about you because he felt you were fragile in some ways, but you had a good heart and he worried that you were softer than them. They are waiting for you outside; your father is outside, and he is standing next to your family. They are all waiting for you."

I could feel him getting off the bed and the feeling that he was eager. At this point I was aware of the boy coming down the stairs and went out the door. I knew that this was Fay. That's the small boy, his younger brother.

I played the song; Hallelujah, which is a song that I have always loved, and the vibration of the song is so deep. My daughter sang this song, and it touches something deep inside me. As I played the song, Angie and I watched Dudley go to the window and peer outside. I held the space for him and allowed my own guardians and light keepers to facilitate the transformation of love shine through. Mr. Newman turned and looked at us and said he would still come visit here. Then he stepped out of the house.

As they faded away, all I can say is that the most amazing feeling of peace came over me. I truly cannot put into words how this is for me. Have you ever had a moment when emotions take over your whole body, maybe overwhelmed with raw grief or joy that you just lose your whole body to crying? Well that is what it feels like. Every emotion that man felt, every feeling and thought, fear and joy, all surges through me and the release of breaking down to the core of who you are all then gives way and there is this peace of just being; just is.

Angie and I followed up with our client and I expressed how the energy of the house will shift and it is very important to raise the vibration of the house with soft music, laughter, candles and sea salt that I sprinkled along the border of the house. I do not always do the same thing and find it funny how there are certain things that I do after this crossing that I do believe is just programmed knowledge within me. But I always have some guidance for my clients afterwards. My feeling is that there will still be some remnants of energy of those spirits and the feeling they may also wander back is a possibility. If the energy of the home is different and not "their" home any longer it feels to me that it helps, ensure they will not be drawn back in. I have no proof of this or really no knowledge to base this on, but more it is my own feeling of something I do.

As I backed out of the driveway of that house, I paused and looked up at this 2-story home. I wished it well and felt such a peaceful feeling of knowing that when I arrived, there was this man inside who was in desperate need of closure, and as I pulled away and drove home, I knew that he was with his family and they were reuniting in a unique way. It is hard to imagine that time has this way of passing and all that you have done in your life can stay with you even in the afterlife. I still at times try to understand the mechanics of death. How the body decays and the shell is shed, but there remains the essence of who we are. All that I am is encapsulated in the unseen energy that goes off into the abyss. It takes with it all the memories, experiences, and thoughts of me, who I was in this life and possibly who I was in all my lives. But some of the memories hold us like an unseen thread that is tethered to the earth's plane and it pulls on us, keeping us not fully free.

I often have wondered if there possibly are several tethered threads connecting us and holding us, thus we are never fully free? Possibly, until we have cut the cord and let go of each of them, are we then fully able to ascend?

I honestly believe that along the known scientific law, that all time co-exists, we must understand that our existence is happening all at once. Many people feel that lives are linear and that live this life and then pass and come back into a brand-new baby. That our lives are about purpose and some designed plan and we come back time and time again until we have mastered that grand plan. I, however, see our existence much like a record that is spinning on a player. Imagine that each record has 10 songs on the album. All the songs are there, and they exist on the record, but you cannot listen to them all at the same time. The needle is your perception and your awareness and where you place the needle down is where your focus and awareness are. But their lives are all happening at the same time. Co-existing all at once. We can move that needle and possibly get a glimpse of lives we may be living, and some may call them those Deja moments, or a heightened awareness of a time spent in another era. This also goes with wondering if our soul, again branched out, like those tethered threads, living these lives that are happening all at once. So, when we pass, there possibly is a lot for us to be letting go of and those tragedies that happen and a sudden death or strong deep rooted emotions of guilt, remorse, obsession and even love hold us back?

There is also this obvious knowing that these emotions have incredible power over us. Our belief of who and what we are has a hold over us that is obviously so deep and can go for hundreds, possibly thousands of years. Omg, what if it can be timeless?

Marguerite and Dudley are two examples of this. Their emotions kept them from knowing that they had the power to let go and move on to find their soulmates, their family and both stayed in their homes where they both died and had tragic deaths.

It also makes me think about how young they both were and really had yet to live their own life and their own identity to some degree. Imagine for a moment that when you are born, you truly take on the role of pleasing people. You are almost programmed from the beginning of time to please people, from your family, siblings, co-worker and boss, possibly all those you have in your circle. You spend a lot of time identifying yourself based on your family dynamics and your experiences. It really is not until you are maybe older and have life experience to possibly begin that journey of self-satisfaction. Think of this time period where your spouses were chosen for you, your life somewhat had been chosen for you, so where was all the time to explore who you really are and what is the core of happiness and joy? I know that some say that it is often in mid-life that many will have this reality hit them with feeling the "OMG, I have lived half of my life and have not done the things I really want to do." That feeling of living more to please the self, then everyone else kicks in. And I also wonder, how did they not see the area of the light and move on with faith and the internal knowing of our existence? It still baffles me. To be honest, it sometimes scares me to think that this is even possible. None of us want to ever be trapped in our own misery. We all know the feeling when you are going through something and you go through it over and over in your mind, like a broken record. How many of you have done that? You have an argument with someone, or some sort of discord and you repeat the conversation, and you go over it, I should have said this, I should have said that, etc.… And we will even say to ourselves that we need to get over it, right?

So, imagine this, you pass away and you are doing this very thing until some medium comes along and snaps her fingers in your face and wakes your ass up! Imagine that for a moment. It is a bit scary to think of.

The Laughing Room

Silver Fountain Inn
Dover, NH

Not every case I work on has a tragic story, some have families that are tied to the property for other reasons. They are places that you may visit now and again and never have known that it is haunted. We always hear about the places that are haunted, the gruesome death or murder, the strange tales of apparitions and legends. But what about the local barbershop, or hardware store, or possibly the quaint bed and breakfast that sits in a beautiful town of Dover, N.H? A place that you would never know had multiple spirits moving about the 3 story Inn, while you sleep or have your morning tea. A place that took me by surprise one afternoon when I was doing that very thing, enjoying a bit of afternoon tea with my wonderful daughter: Nicole.

Nicole moved to Dover several years ago on Silver Street. What an amazing street this was, several beautiful Victorian homes with unique farmer porches, some small and quaint and some grand, wrapping about the home. Each home is as breathtaking as the next one and they all line Silver Street. I can recall her saying several times as we drove by the Silver Fountain Inn, that she was drawn to that Inn and some day we must go check it out. At the time we didn't realize just how wonderful the Inn was and all the delights it has to offer.

Nicole began to do some research and called me one evening. Her excitement bubbling over as it often has. The Inn offered a Victorian High Tea Luncheon. There were several reservation times to choose from and we could make reservations and have lunch together. What a delightful idea, to come visit her and have a girl's day! I'll be over tomorrow I told her, so sign us up.

The Inn is breathtaking. If you ever wanted to step back into the Victorian era, this is the place to visit.

We sat in the small dining room, a room full of flower tapestries, vases of hydrangeas, roses, lilies and many of the old fashion Victorian garden flowers. The tables were set for an elegant luncheon, assorted china pieces, each as delicate and as the next one. Pam, the owner is very delightful. Her energy exudes her enjoyment of her home and business.

Silver Fountain Inn

She greeted us and sat us at a table that faced the main entrance of the Inn.

The view of the outdoor gardens and the water fountain could be seen from our window. Off to the right was a doorway that led to the main entrance with an amazing grand staircase. During our entire lunch I was just enchanted with the doorway and staircase and I must be truthful that I wanted to just get up and go explore and wander the Inn. This happens to me often at locations I visit where I just am "called" to go explore and many times I have done that with my children or family reminding me that I can't just go walk into areas that are not for customers. I must tell you that it is hard to resist. I knew someone was calling me and it did not take too long before a very young-looking woman dressed in a long sort of plain jane dress appeared in the doorway, standing alongside her was a young boy. She had brown hair all pulled up high on top of her head. She had a simple elegance about her, but I truly got the impression that this was a place she lived at. The Inn had a homey feeling about it to her. She just looked at me as to say hello and then slowly faded away.

So here we go, and I knew that Nicole wanted to explore this place. She was drawn to it from the moment she moved in across the street. I told her that I would reach out to Pam and see what she said about doing an investigation here. When I find these locations, well they do seem to call to me, and I try to create an event that keeps the character of the location intact. A beautiful Victorian Inn does not want to be known as a "haunted destination". There are many locations that enjoy the title, but many are doing quite well with the reputation they have worked so hard to create.

I sent Pam an introduction email about myself and what I do, along with the idea of doing some sort of event that would allow me to come enjoy the Inn, but also open its doors to the public in maybe a unique way. She was delighted and yes, really wanted to not have the Inn known as a haunted Inn, but was also very interested in who was residing in the Inn, as the staff and guests have had an encounter or two. We created a psychic fair with readers and vendors, a high noon luncheon followed by an evening overnight investigation. It was the perfect event for the beautiful 3 story Inn.

Imagine having a home that you poured your heart and soul into, you wander the halls and go about your life, without ever being noticed by those around you? Just imagine this. The ghost of a man who walks his home without ever making eye contact with those around him. This is very much the story of this location. The Inn was not a strong paranormal location with things being moved, lights going on and off, but more a soft feeling of a presence that may be lingering in your room, or the smell of roses that all of a sudden fills the room. No one would know that the Silver Fountain Inn was haunted, unless you had that little beam of light that seems to shine around sensitive people.

Oh, she sees me, so I am going to make myself known to her. Literally, I felt a man follow me around that entire day. I could feel him just standing a breaths distance away from my shoulder. I knew he was tall and lanky. Not a robust man but more a solid tall presence behind me. I did not see him at first but could hear him talking, wanting to show me his home. He made me look at the ceilings in the dining room and how they were a pleasure for him. He brought me upstairs and made me look at all the wood crown molding that seemed very artistically designed. I could feel his pride and hard work. This man loved his home and had a real interest in showing me it. Occasionally, I could see this man's facial expressions. He had a squarish face with a high forehead and often was wearing a hat of some sort, which he would take off and sort of nod his head to say hello to me. He seemed to have a mustache or facial hair like a goat tee of some sort. I could not quite tell exactly but knew he had a mustache of some sort. He had a very gentle energy about him, like a man that had not only a lot of wisdom but kindness.

My room for the night was the suite and it had this noticeably light heartedness feel about it. The entire Inn had this feeling. There was not that oppressive heavy feeling in the chest like you truly need to take a breath, as many locations often have. This one was a very subtle lighthearted, almost warm feeling to the atmosphere.

As the day continued, there was a woman that showed herself to me and talked to me in the formal dining room. Every time she was around, my stomach hurt like I had a corset on or some sort of restricted mid-section. I felt she was very tiny and very petite compared to the gentleman that was following me around.

Many times, I was drawn across the street and felt this pull of someone showing me more ownership or property that was with this Inn. I did not get the feeling that this was an Inn back in its day but was this man's home and possibly he owned the whole street or the area around the Inn. However, the houses on the street were incredibly old, so it was a bit confusing as to what he owned, and he kept making me feel there was more. I felt they were very hard workers, they tended to their property very much in the same way Pam and her husband do. You can tell a lot about the pride someone has in their home by their landscape and it does not always have to be done professionally. A little hard work can go a long way with curb appeal. This was the feeling I got from this man and woman.

Main Dining Room

They did not seem to be here for any pressing issue, rather enjoying living in their home in the afterlife just as they had before. I sensed they came and went, possibly when someone comes admiring the woodwork and fine décor, this man may just pop in to see who is staying at his home. I did not get the feeling they needed anything from me other than just wanting to show me around. They both referred to being incredibly happy with Pam and her husband and very much enjoyed having the Inn welcoming of people. It felt like this was a community man and this home had people also being entertained.

My room on both occasions that I have held this event was called the Brown Room. Each time a group of us would wander into this room to do some communications, to find ourselves laughing hysterically for no reason at all. I am talking about laughing to the point you are going to wet your pants and your belly hurts so bad! All I can think of is that maybe this room was a happy place for someone or a gathering of some sort.

Music could be heard on and off in a few of the rooms. You could hear the soft sounds of a piano subtly playing within the walls. I always felt comfortable here, like a warm welcome greeted me as I walked throughout the Inn.

The night before the event I stayed alone at the Inn. It was such a cool experience to have the entire Inn all to myself. Pam lives above the Carriage house, which is also on the property, located behind the parking lot. So here I am alone in the Inn, with delicious tea that I can make at any time I wish. If you are a connoisseur of tea, this is the place to go to. She has hundreds of tea blends to choose from. I am not an avid tea drinker but have to say the biscotti tea is delicious. I made myself a pot of tea and took it to my room. Of course, I had to explore a bit. I took my cup and wandered around. Each floor had a little quaint sitting area at the base of each staircase. I sat at the 2nd floor sitting area enjoying the quietness. I could see the faint swoosh of energy pass by from room to room. That is the best way I can describe it, a swoosh. There was not always a solid apparition that would be seen, but a swoosh of energy that just passed by. I felt very much like the Inn was busy, energies that were not necessarily aware of me or wanting to be aware of me, but more doing their thing. There was a strong feeling of servants or staff that came from the 3rd floor. It felt like the man and woman were mainly on the second floor, like this was their rooms or where they spent a lot of time. I was not sure if possibly the first floor was for entertaining or possibly maybe they ran an Inn of some sort or business out of the main floor. I could not quite tell why most of their energy felt very much on the second floor.

As I sat, there was a woman who kept coming around and she was quite different from the other woman who I had met. This woman had an elegance about her. She had a bit of an ownership feeling also. She wanted me to know she had her heart here and that she felt she did not want to leave. Like she needed to be there for some reason. She seemed happy and enjoyed coming and going from the home, again checking in. After communicating with her, she told me that she lived here, and this was her home. She came from across the way and needed to be here. She had a loneliness when she told me this, like this woman was the sole survivor of the home, the madam of the house, so to speak. She showed me the gardens and kept showing me the side of the house, a small sitting area sat under a tree. Was this a place she sat or had a fondness of? I did not know, but she kept taking me there. I would stand there and look and wonder, okay what is she showing me?

I made my way back to my room and felt very much like I was tucked in my bed. Literally, I felt a woman come in and sort of tuck me in bed. The woman with the tight chest. I could see her dress and the silhouette of her face. She came into the room and then faded away. This room was so comforting to sleep in and the bed itself was like sinking into a big pile of comfy down blankets.

Frank and Mary Williams

After I learned the history of the Inn, which was so wonderful to not only have validation of my feelings and experiences but knowing that this was in fact a family home was priceless.

The Inn was built in 1871 and was by Frank and Mary Williams. Frank was the very tall man with a large handlebar mustache and an immensely proud father and businessman in his community. He worked alongside his father's building the I. B. Williams & Sons Manufacturing Co. His father, himself and George built a business in lace and belt-making into one of the largest successful businesses in Dover, NH.

The factory was originally located in the Cocheco Mills which was a prosperous mill in the area. He was immensely proud of his family and business and it showed not only in the records, but also in his spirit which was so eager to discuss this.

His wife, Mary and his two daughters, Marguerite and Dorothy both lived in the home for many years. Mary was described as a very loving and petite woman, mind you with a small waistline. I could not help but look at the picture that Pam showed me and observe her tiny features.

Marguerite, who spelled out her name with the dowsing rods to several guests during the night's investigation, lived across the street, which she also pointed the rods in that direction. She lived in what is now a residence, however, her home after her living there, had become the Old Gaol, (jail) where it is known as the last public hanging in Dover. Just imagine the stories that location could tell. That may be a future story to tell for sure.

Dorothy resided in the house next door and often visits the house to this day. She moved back into the home when her husband and parents all passed. I truly felt she felt close to her family and wants to continue visiting her childhood home even in her spirit years.

As I read about the history of this home, it was no wonder that Frank and Mary were guiding me throughout the home. They were a family of wealth and had pride in their home.

What I learned about the home was that wealth and image was everything. From the Italian intricate carved plaster ceiling, mahogany doors and woodwork, imported Belgian light fixtures, large sandstone fireplaces, hand-cut crystal doorknobs and beautiful cabinetry with secret hiding places. This Inn is too hard to describe, it is one you must see for yourself to understand the beauty.

When entering the home, you are welcomed by the staff, which would have been a significant number to keep this grand home well maintained for the family and any guests visiting. There was a modest kitchen, pantry, several dining and sitting rooms.

There was a music room where guests and family may have been delightfully entertained after dinner.

The second floor was where the family bedrooms and personal dressing rooms were, with the 3rd floor housing the servants, which may have consisted of a butler and a few chambermaids and women who prepared the meals for the family. What always is interesting when I visit these homes, is that you can always tell where the hired help lived, as the grandness and décor become quite simple.

What did I learn from the Silver Fountain Inn? What I learned was that many locations simply have activity that is not with a tale of some dark folklore, unsolved deaths, emotions that are hindering the spirits from moving on, but the total opposite. A location that many of the family members visit because it holds a piece of their heart and soul. Often this has made me ponder the reality that we leave our essence, we leave literally our DNA scattered throughout the foundation of a home. Is it possible that DNA particles can draw us back? A medium comes along and touches, or possibly breaths in these particles and can summon us back. Summon us back for a reunion to some degree? This family is happy to come and go and thus each year I will enjoy strolling their beautiful Inn with tea in hand, a moment to honor their legacy and story to share.

The Shadow Man

Private Residence

Fitchburg, MA

This case brings me way back to the same year that I had gone to the Shanley. This was another part of my beginning development of understanding my spirit ways.

I had just published The Mirror Magazine and truly was enjoying the writing and creating of each page. I surprised myself as I was now the publisher of a digital magazine. Who would have thought? As I said in the beginning, if you put your mind to something, well you will be amazed what you can do.

I wanted to get insight from a panel of people in the field. I wanted to ask a series of questions about spirituality, ghosts, spirits, communications and just some random questions on the matter. I thought okay, I will ask a few readers, a few paranormal investigators and a few random people all the same questions and see the different answers they give. It was just a shout out on Facebook to see who may be willing to participate. I had a paranormal team that I thought was very interesting in their responses and just had a little bit of a nudge to reach out and see about interviewing the team and maybe even joining them on an investigation to feature the team and their style, motives, and passion for the field.

This brought me to a home in Fitchburg, MA. This home was quite the learning experience for me and looking back to this day, still leaves me with questions.

What started as a simple observation and writing about the team's evening investigation, turned into the spirits of the home communicating with me while I was in the home and making me realize the severity this family needed. They needed far more than a paranormal team establishing whether the house was haunted. Do not get me wrong, there are many paranormal teams that exist, and each have their own abilities and purpose. Some are deeply passionate about the science of investigating; some are more interested in the documentation of poltergeist activity or historical pieces to study and write about. There are also many that are a combination of teams that work with only tech geeks, as we call ourselves, and others working with mainly psychics and mediums and some a combination of both. There are many that are designed for the documentation of paranormal activity and love to do full research and help the homeowner with validation and documentations, however, many do not truly stay on to assist in the resolving. I have come across this time and time again, and there is nothing wrong with these teams, aside from many that project their views onto the home owners and some not fully honorable in what they deem in a home truly can affect the homeowner's belief systems and reality. Investigators all go home and do not have to live in the home they have now stirred up or deemed something bad is happening. I could write for hours just on this topic. It is why I always try to tell people to first seek out a team that understands what you need. If you feel you need to have the situation in your home resolved, then a team that is just interested in documenting, will not have the ability to truly help and may in fact cause more problems as spirits who need assistance, get even more frustrated to be mocked or continued to be unheard. Some places, like the Silver Fountain Inn and other locations I have worked on, the owner just wants to understand who is haunting their home or business and are not having serious paranormal issues. So, teams to document are great for this. Just depends on your overall purpose.

When I walked into the home, I immediately felt this incredible heavy energy from the entire house. I entered a small mud/laundry room and felt overall okay this is a very active place. Immediately there was the presence of a little girl and she seemed to be hiding. I felt this feeling of sadness hit me and there is a little girl here that is in pain, that something terrible happened to her. It hit me to the core.

As I walked through the home, there was a room to my left that had a slider leading out to the back yard. This room had an overpowering feeling of anger. I felt a man standing in the corner and at the time did not see him enough to describe him but again, I could feel his presence just staring at me. I could feel the anger in his being and thought okay this is going to be an interesting location. I then made my way to the stairs to go up to the bedrooms, which their two children occupied. As soon as I stood at the base of the staircase, it was this heavy dense air that literally felt like it was pushing against me, almost seeming to keep me from climbing the stairs. Once upstairs, it was immediate with the nausea and headache and sickening feeling. A very heavy strong presence was up there, and it creeped me out. I couldn't identify a male or woman but just knew that whoever it was, its energy was in the entire 2nd floor, which mainly consisted of 2 bedrooms and a bathroom, with a center open room and a door that led outside, however the door was bored as it was a door to nowhere. The owner was doing many renovations.

We decided to sit in the center room area where we could see into all the rooms from this angle. I sat with my back against the wall and the rooms were to my left. It was dark in the area, but the outside moonlight was shining through the windows enough to illuminate the upstairs.

As I sat there, which seemed to not be exceptionally long at all, I looked over into the daughter's room. I was looking directly at the window in the room and just looking at the room, feeling drawn to it. And there it was, a large shadow of at least 7 feet tall slowly moving from one side of the room to the other, totally blocking the window and all light that was coming in. It cleared the room and faded into the closet. My eyes never moved from watching it and my skin was feeling clammy. What the hell did I just see? This was my first visual shadow like this. I know that sounds strange coming from me who saw Marguerite and other spirits, but this was the first time seeing a large shadow move like this and seeing it clearly with my physical eyes. I went into the room and truly felt like this is more powerful than we think and not going to be easy. I just knew it.

After our discussions with what we were feeling in the home, the owner reached out to me personally and wanted me to come back to her house and take it over myself. I remember feeling when we left that night and I am sure she saw it in my eyes as I felt that okay, what do we do now? This team had been working on her house for some time and not sure where they stood, but I felt like okay we need to talk to these spirits and we need to know who they are and what to do for them so this family can rest at night.

And so, it began with me returning to the home, a home that had it all. It had true poltergeist activity, angry spirits, with intense power, and in the mix a loving presence that wanted to hug you and make things safe and better.

This house I had some insight going in as I had known some of the situations the family had been dealing with. The brief insight I had was that the owner had inherited the home from her grandmother, which she was very close with and delighted to have the opportunity to have a home of her own for her wife and her wife's 2 children; a son and daughter. The home had been in the family since the 1900's and you could tell she had a lot of pride with ambitions of renovating the home and making more her own, but also truly valued the history of the home. She didn't realize when she inherited the house that it was going to be full of spirits with a lot of stored anger and hostility.

When I met with the owner, we sat outside enjoying the warm summer evening. She had a great backyard with an above ground pool, gazebo screen house which was all lit up with twinkle lights. A girl after my own heart. I loved her warm and welcoming personality and truly a sweet loving person with a heart of gold. You could tell her character right away; she wore it on her sleeve. She was honest and upfront and has a genuine angelic quality about her, but don't get me wrong, she is also someone who will tell you to go take a jump off a cliff if you burn her. What I liked about her was that she was honest and did not have some agenda. She would give you the shirt off her back and her very heart, but do not mess with her emotions and don't be hurtful or deceptive. She trusted everyone, and she was opening her home to me; truly a total stranger and she was about to tell me her deepest fears and insecurities. She was nervous I would judge her and that is the mortal sin in her eyes and would break her. She was at her wits end and trying to hold her family together. She had the pressure of trying to figure so much out in her own life and her own family dynamics, along with her wife's family dynamics and inheriting a house of hell, as she worded it. This all was beginning to be a heavy load and the scales of happiness were tipping to places she really did not want to have occurred at this point in her life.

We sat for what felt like hours and she told me so many things that were happening in the house. She and her wife were continually woken up in their room with the presence of a dark shadow man standing at the foot of the bed, swearing at them and saying horrible things like they were going to rot in hell. Her wife was punched in the stomach on one occasion and pushed down the stairs on another. Her wife's paranoia getting the best of her and at times refusing to come out of the bedroom as the "thing" was in the kitchen. Often the kitchen appliances would come on randomly and things on the counters knocked off and thrown on the floor. Imagine sleeping in at night and hearing this in the kitchen and not knowing what would happen if you got up to go check. They both would see this dark shadow come through the living room and kitchen and go down into the basement, which is located just off the kitchen. Both would just freeze in fear to not disturb it and let it go about its business. They were terrified of whatever it was.

She had told me on several occasions she would see the cross that she had hanging, a cross that came with the house, hanging just on the wall next to the basement door, swaying and moving. A family member took the cross to get rid of. Then the family member started to have problems and brought the cross back. So back it was on the wall and my client not knowing what to do with it.

She told me how both the children were having issues and seeing this shadow coming in and out of their room and the entire household was continually arguing and on edge. She felt like both the children's behavior and personality were changing and not for the better.

She had told me one day she was on the couch downstairs and her son came down the stairs sort of with this scowl on his face and looking very bizarre in his mannerism. She asked him what the matter and he was screamed at her. She got up and was approaching him, like what the hell is wrong with you and never talk to me like that again. She faced him and felt, this is not her son and she knew at that point if she said anything more, he would probably beat the crap out of her. He had a look of hatred and pure evil in his eyes and it frightened her. My client is a big woman, she could probably push anyone over with her finger, and her son was also a broad shoulder large kid for his age, so her saying this made me see the severity of the situation. Something was for sure going on in this house to affect the family so dramatically.

She gave me a set of keys and told me to come and go if it took to figure out what was going on in her home and to get rid of it. I explained my process and felt the need to take this on to the best of my ability and if I needed help, I would find it.

I pulled up one brutal winter day, with my dowsing rods and flashlights in hand. At the time this is all I used for communication, and of course myself, but this was the main gadget that I used. I also had my recorder going in case I captured any EVP's of anyone in the house. This was not my focus, but it never hurts to have these items just in case. To this day it still sends shivers up my back when I hear a voice of a spirit I am communicating with on my recorder. It is somehow an extra level of validation. The tool I use now is an SLS connect which shows the spirit in a stick figure often standing next to me.

So, I entered the home and still felt that immediate rush of energy entering the home. I set my stuff in the kitchen and felt a warm sensation come over me and was drawn back to the entrance area, which was the mud/laundry room. I decided to sit down on the floor and listen.

There was the presence of a beautiful energy here and she was so loving and caring. She made me feel warm and began to touch my arm, which you will see the picture of her hand touching my arm. It shows up as this greenish mist. I did not feel scared at all but more like she was welcoming me to her home and had a sigh of relief that I was here. She went on to tell me she was trying extremely hard to protect everyone and that she loved her home. I got this immediate feeling she was a woman who endured a lot in life, and she talked about how there was abuse in the home and she tried to do her best. She also was trying to do her best in her afterlife here in the home. I felt such sincerity with her and man, this was hard because I felt like all I wanted to do was sit with her and tell her it was going to be okay, but honestly I didn't feel like she was going to leave the house. She was not stuck there, but she took on the protector role of the home even in the afterlife. I felt she was also trying to show me or somehow make me aware of a little spirit of a girl that was continually hiding in the home. She was also trying to protect her. The little girl never communicated with me and honestly, I was not fully sure who she was as when I would get a glimpse of her and begin to tune into her, she would vanish.

Okay, so let us explore the home a bit and see what is going on here and just what this woman spirit is protecting the homeowners from. I was then drawn to the room again that led out to the outdoor pool area. Immediately as I entered the room, again the presence of man was there, and he was showing me the slider and how he normally looked out that area. He was more receptive to me this visit. He was upset that this was his room that he appeared to spend time in, and they have destroyed it. I got the strong sense that this was his home, and he was upset at the handling of it. He went on to tell me how much he hated what they were doing. He identified himself as being the owner of the home and in fact this was Harvey, my client's grandfather. He was not a nice man, and he told me yes, he was abusive and had struggles with alcohol and smoked. He hacked and coughed and the entire time I was with him, my chest felt so tight. He wanted to show me what "they had done". Okay, show me! He led me to the basement. He was terribly angry that they changed part of the basement. "Harvey, well this is your granddaughter and it's her home now and she will make changes." But he was so bitter about this. In his eyes he still owned the home and how dare they do this. I had set up flashlights, one for yes and one for no, which often spirits will use to answer questions so I can get more documentation than in my head. He had no problem using the flashlights to answer many questions. It was like he wanted to talk and tell me all that he had going on. He had confirmed who he was and that he owned this home, and he had a lot of pride in the home. He didn't agree with the lifestyle that his granddaughter lived. This is what was always hard for me to fully grasp. It was okay that he beat his wife and family, and sorry to be so honest, but that he could do this, but it was not okay for a woman to fall in love with another woman and marry her? So yes, this was a huge problem for him. He had a vileness about him a bit with this and truly deemed my client not being worthy of owning his home.

I asked Harvey a lot of questions about many things. I wanted to understand the process of death. Did he see where he was supposed to go or could choose to go, and he said he could see it. I asked him several times this question and he always answered that he knew he passed, and he knew where he could go, but he wanted to stay. He was choosing to stay. Hmmm, so do we all have that ability? Do we all see the light or area that we can go to, but we choose to not for our own reasons, whether fear, doubt, guilt and all the other reasons one may decide to not. Man, if they only knew that they could go there and still check in from time to time with their home or family. But it leaves that question of what their beliefs are about that "place" or "light" that is there. I suppose if you feel you are not worthy to go there, then you will not. If you honestly believe there is a hell, then why would you chance it?

But Harvey was clear he was choosing to stay because he did not want to let go of his home. As I write this I think, man he chose that over all the possibilities of his own spiritual evolution. Believe me I talked to him about his very thing and that he can leave the house. This man was also pretty set in his ways and I do think that he had doubts about possibly the character he had deep inside and was possibly worried that he would not like where he thought he may end up.

He was clear in his emotions and purpose here and I thought okay, well what do we do with you? I got a sense from him that possibly I will be able to soften him a bit and maybe compromise on maybe my client honoring some areas and deem them as "his" areas? I was not yet sure just how this was going to go, and I also knew he may be the one standing over their bed saying awful things, but this was not the only energy in the home. I expressed to him my purpose of being here and that I also will make sure that my clients respect his boundary, but he has to also respect their boundary or that I would be forced to be the bigger bully as they say. I know he understood me.

You see, you can't just go in and make spirits who are what many may say in limbo leave. Honestly, it totally goes against every spiritual, compassionate, human quality that we have under all our layers. It also goes against just about every religious belief system that I have studied. It troubles me that so many religious belief systems are about loving and accepting humanity, and the whole concept of forgiveness and seeking attunement, however, it only really applies if you conform to what that religion deems to be worthy. It is totally ass backwards in my view, because deep within us is our soul and the soul is not for humans to judge or rule over. That is what every religion deems as God's will. So, if it is God's will, then how can you turn your back on anyone? Believe me this case as we dive into it, even challenged me to have to dig deep within my own belief systems. Can I do the very same thing?

So here I am making a connection with Harvey, but I did not feel that he was the only one that was causing the intensity of the paranormal activity in the home.

I made my way to the stairs but let me tell you all areas of the home had this feeling of activity. It is a bit hard to explain. Many times, some spirits will sort of reside in an area, and you may feel their energy more in that area. Yes, they like us move about, but the core of their energy may reside in a certain spot. I guess if you look at your home and what areas of the home you spend most of your time in, that may actually have a lot of residual energy in it, even the smell of your hair or perfume or cologne that you wear. It lingers. Other times there is this feeling that the entire house has energy, like walking into a home that is heavily haunted with more than one spirit and depending on how many, well you can feel it like walking into a crowded room. This house very much felt like this. I was walking into a crowded room.

I made my way to the staircase again and went up into the rooms, each of the rooms had a feel to it. I got very emotional in the daughter's room. Her bed was covered with stuffed animals, with a pink typical girly bedspread. As I sat in this room, I felt such a sadness and lost innocence that I wasn't quite sure I fully understood. The entire time I was upstairs I could feel the presence of the shadow man. I must call him that for now because I did not know who he was, but I saw his shadow and knew it was a male. I could feel his energy totally on the 2nd floor and truly felt he resided here the most. He creeped me out and felt him always just standing behind me or above me, with a denseness to him. A feeling of power, dominance and anger coming from him. I did not like being upstairs in the house and I could tell that these kids did not either. It felt like their rooms were just to sleep and get the hell out. They had their rooms decorated, yes, with personality to them, but they were so unkept and had an empty feeling about them.

This shadow man would not talk to me and I could feel him totally assessing me, maybe sizing me up. I walked about and talked out loud and told him why I was here. I felt the presence of other energies in the home, but I could not separate them out. This shadow man was clouding the whole upstairs and to some degree front and center stage.

Okay, so this may be a few visits for sure to get this man to relax and possibly allow me to not only see him but have him talk to me. I was a bit perplexed but not surprised because sometimes the energies that are intense can do two things, they either will come at you with all their emotions and issues or they will wait to do just what I had said, assess me and my motive and character. I also do feel they know deep down my purpose; I always feel that spirits can see far deeper into you than you think. It is why it is so important to be careful if you have deep inner demons of your own or insecurities that make you very vulnerable. I have seen it time and time again with people who investigate and open themselves up to spirit communications when they themselves have a lot of emotional baggage or inner conflicts, drug or alcohol excessive use or psychological and depression tendencies. It just makes them so vulnerable and live bait for some spirits that prey on weaker souls. So many people are strong on the outside to the world, but inside they are not and well in my personal opinion, the paranormal world is great to learn from, but some locations and places are not the best for them to visit or live in.

Simply stated, when you live with demons, you see demons everywhere you go, when you live with angels, you see angels everywhere you go. It is what you do not see that can bite you in the ass. You must be grounded spiritually, mentally and have above all a strong inner sense of self to do this work.

So many people ask me if I get scared at all, and honestly, I do not. It is kind of weird for me, as I may watch scary movies and get creeped out just like anyone else. I can recall a few times watching a scary movie and lying in bed trying to not think about it. How funny that is, right? But yes, movies scare me too. The actual haunted house does not seem to. I just have this sort of inner knowing in me that whatever is in the home I will just be able to deal with.

So, on my first visit, I got a good grasp of Harvey and the Grandmother. The little girl never appeared enough for me to have a conversation with her, and there were several energies that I felt coming and going, but not fully residing in the home. The Shadow man was going to be tricky as he was not being very receptive to me and just continued to observe me but not engage. During one of my visits, my daughter Nicole assisted me. She was now very much wanting to also understand her own abilities, as she too, like my son, Garrett have had experiences of their own. She felt the presence of him as soon as we went upstairs. We stood in the center area of the second floor. This visit I was now beginning to feel him possibly willing to speak. Nicole was standing just behind me. "Sam", he said in her ear, causing Nicole to jump towards me. He clearly said his name very loudly and clearly right in her ear. She felt she could almost feel his breath on her neck, which scared the hell out of her. She was a bit shaken by this as we went into the daughter's room and sat on the bed. Nicole began to videotape me, while I was talking to him, she could see this small illuminating orb slowly moving all around me. She was seeing it visually with her own eyes, as well as it was clearly on our video camera. As I began to talk to "Sam", he started to show himself to me. He was a big man, with a bit of what I would describe as a typical beer belly. He was messy looking and had a disheveled look about him. He stood just next to me, like any moment he would overpower me if he could. I was straight forward with him. "You don't scare me, Sam", I would say out loud to him.

He was a spirit that enjoyed intimidation and being a dominant force. This was surely not a spirit to have in your home. His energy I could tell was pure anger and bitterness.

At this point, I felt it may be a good idea to sit with the son and daughter to hear their viewpoint of what they were feeling and explain a little more about what I was doing there. The owner explained they were not just terrified, but they wanted to meet me personally and understand for themselves what was going on. I can totally understand their interest in meeting me, especially with both seeing and feeling the activity in the home, well, I wish someone sat with me when I was that age and helped me understand.

Nicole joined me during this visit, which may have also helped with the whole teenage shyness and I am sure felt uneasy telling a total stranger their problems. They both, however, were open with me. The daughter began with feeling like she was never alone in the house and often saw a shadow of a man move across her room. She would see it go into her closet and feels generally uneasy upstairs. She hears things moving around in her closet and an ice-cold breeze comes in and out of her bedroom. She has had the feeling that the energy follows her to school, and she has a hard time focusing. When she goes to her father's house, as her parents are divorced, she doesn't feel the same feelings as she does in the house.

The son feels the same sort of thing and he also sees a dark shadow that stands at the foot of his bed. A glowing light has been seen coming down from the ceiling by his closet which scared the hell out of him. He tries hard to not focus on it, but he feels like he cannot at times and feels like he used to be a normal teenager until they moved into this house. He has fits of anger and sadness that he does not understand. He dreams of extremely negative and weird things. He knows it is not him as he generally does not have that much anger inside of him.

Both the kids described to me that they lived in an apartment before moving into this house and they were a happy family, playing games and hanging out together, and now since they live here, well they all seem to fight nonstop and there is this thing that they feel is changing them all.

As we sat in the kitchen, I truly felt so much for these two kids. I tried to talk to them about spirit energy and who and what it often is and explained my purpose to understand and help the spirits as much as help them. I explained all that I do and the reasons for it. I also talked about being a medium and what it was like as a teenager and really appreciated both of them feeling they could trust me and by all means talk opening to me about all the crazy things going on.

Nicole and I left that evening with a bit of a heavy heart. I still clearly recall, Nicole turning to me as we got in the car and saying, "Mom, we have to help these people." That became the mission and believe me it was not easy to get this one shadow energy to open up to me. I believe we had gone to the house at least 6 times before, he finally revealed to me who he was.

Each visit I would go and talk to Harvey and the grandmother and one remarkably interesting thing was that the grandmother would often show herself in a green mist that would swirl around your body.

Green Mist (photo brightened so you can see better)

The team that I had interviewed had shown me pictures of the green mist that they had captured during one of their investigations. At first when you look at the pictures, you see what looks like the head of a snake with its body entangling the owner. It was quite freaky to be honest and someone would more than likely this day in age label that a demon, because of the creepiness of the picture. But if they only knew that this was the grandmother and she would try to surround who she was around with loving healing energy, which just so happens to be green. She was the green mist that I met and touched my arm the first visit and this is the green mist that more than likely was the ball of light that Nicole was seeing swirl all around me when she was videotaping me in the daughter's bedroom. We did not take pictures, but I would place a bet on it that this green mist would have been there.

I learned in this home that many energies manifest in different ways, and you cannot deem them good, evil, demon or any of the sort by how they manifest. Some present as a shadow, and some a green mist or a cloudy mist, orbs and partial or full body apparitions. Some also present with a smell, which can be anything from their favorite perfume or cologne, cigars, body order and even pot roast smells. Yes, pot roast as that is one of the spirits at the Conjuring house's way of presenting herself sometimes. The best thing to do is just take notes and document but do not determine if the spirit is evil or good based on it being a shadow or orb.

It started as a boy, his hatred for women, he said. He was just a little boy and his mom used to bring him sometimes to this house, but it was not the house as it is now. He felt dragged there and saw horrific things happen in this home, some of which I really cannot write about, but the things men did to his mom, was just indescribable for a young boy. I also got the feeling that possibly, his mother allowed things to be done to her son, something that I had the most difficult time viewing as a medium. This is when being a medium and being able to see the horrific things that have happened to people is sometimes why I escape to my solitude and away from people, as much as I am a people person, my work shows me quite a lot and I need a break from it from time to time. He endured a lot as a child and grew up having a bitter taste in his mouth for women and people in general. He showed me that this grew in him and he took his anger out on many in the area. I truly could see him sort of prowling the neighborhood and visiting homes along the way. What was hard to fully grasp was that this seemed like he was the same in spirit as he was when living. I knew he visited possibly many of the homes in this neighborhood and potentially several homes may in fact be haunted by this same "Shadow man" that identified himself as Sam.

Sam told me he worked in the mill behind the home, a mill that many of the people he worked with would have had no idea the capability of this man. We hear it all the time, oh that man was the nicest man, and kept to himself, while he is being arrested for mutilating animals or murdering someone. This seemed to be the alias that Sam had, the guy that worked in the mill and no one would ever think anything of the sort. I truly felt he was a child molester, and he did not argue this point with me as he showed me images of his life. This was hard for me and helped explain why he was so drawn to the upstairs of the house and really resided there the most. That was where my client's children spent most of their time, in their bedrooms and middle area where they did their homework. Sam was feeding off children and possibly trying to torment them the same way he did when he was a living man. I can remember so clearly, telling Sam that if he was alive, I would have no problem shooting him dead. I am just being brutally honest, that I am a compassionate person and understand the evil of man, but I am also a mother and human being and it would be very hard to not judge this man and his actions.

I sat in a sort of emptiness state of nothing that day at the house. I began to cry for him as a boy, seeing what he endured and understanding where his anger and hatred formed. I mourned for him as a child who should never have endured what his mother exposed him to. I think this is why he began to show me his life and talk to me, as he saw that I could try my best to listen to him and allow him to really tell me who he was. I was very truthful with him as I cried. I mourned with him a bit his youth, but I also was so not accepting the choices he made and told him this. That he had choices to become the man he was or something better. I was angry with him and he understood this. I also told him that I had to protect the family from his behavior if he was going to continue to harm this family and that I would have to force him out of the home if it came down to it. He had this chilling laugh that sent chills down my spine. I knew this was a challenge and was not 100% sure exactly what I was dealing with. How to deal with the real evil that man does, that was a question I had for myself as I told Sam I needed to take a break and clear my head a bit. I asked him to respect my wishes and leave the family alone and that I would return.

I drove home that day in a fog. How can I do this? How can I have compassion for a man who did these awful things to children! Regardless of what happened to himself as a child. I think this case truly was a turning point in my paranormal work because one must ask themselves this very question. How can you help anyone if you judge them? And who am I to judge the soul and spirit of a person. Yes, I can judge and have opinions in my heart with the living, the actions that people do, but I am not God and, in some ways,, I have not walked in this man's shoes. Do I have enough in my heart to help him, forgive him, and help him find peace? I knew that I needed to know that within myself because how dare I do this work of helping lost souls find peace if I judge. Oh wait, no your soul should not be helped because I am going to determine that based on my small human mind that means nothing in the vastness of the Universe. Who am I to do this work and be a hypocrite if I cannot help all of mankind? I think for any of us, this is when your true character can be tested.

Imagine you are at the grocery store and you see an elderly man or woman struggling with their shopping bags. You immediately would help, right? Oh, let me help you with your bags. This a natural human emotion that we have inside us. But what if you knew that man or woman was a child molester? Or abusive and did awful things? Would you still help? It's a sticky wicket I know. Because now we are in the realm of our moral code. Is our moral code the same for everyone and every circumstance? This is what I was facing with this case. Who am I really? What is my character underneath it all? Empathy is Empathy and it has not a face.

Silas Pratt began to build on the property in 1897, a piece of property that had a small dwelling overlooking the town. The property sat at the top of a hill and overlooked the Mill and town. What I discovered through research is that every person that lived in the home from 1897 to current day, has experienced some form of domestic violence and alcoholism. The property had a series of arrest reports, prostitution, drug and even a murder/suicide with the most bizarre turn of events. It seemed that everyone that lived in the home suffered on some level, both physical trauma and mental trauma.

Is it possible that a piece of property can become haunted, not only with the spirits that may be residing in it, but the actual energy of the events that have gathered on a property over time? It made me wonder if each family moved into the home, was somehow absorbing the past trauma and history of the property, along with being affected by the spirits that are lingering for their own purpose. One of the interesting things about this property was that I could identify certain spirits that were still lingering and could work with them to help resolve the reason they are there, but there were people coming and going in the home

also. It felt like the house had a lot of residual energy that was coming
and going and possibly many of the energies that once traveled in and
out of this house back in its time, somehow like an old movie projector
playing over and over the same clip. It was odd. My feelings were truly
that this house may always be active and one would have to work hard
to establish boundaries and change the whole energetic field.

In my communications what I had learned from Harvey truly was
amazing insight. I learned that we have choices and that quite possibly,
we move on when we are good and ready. Harvey was clear of his
wanting to be in his home and what troubled him was that he was
an abusive man while living. He confirmed in an EVP when asked if
there was domestic violence in the home, he replied, "There was some."
We all heard this clearly. He also felt this was his home and he was
not happy with his granddaughter making changes. What was most
troubling though was that he had a very mean and angry view towards
her way of life. Harvey considering himself a Christian man, struggled
with his granddaughter being married to a woman. I am sure this was
the main source of his bitterness as he would stand over their bed with
awful hatred and often verbal assaults that could be heard clearly. He
needed to understand that this was her home now and regardless of
his views, he was not living anymore, and she actually was making
incredible structural changes to the home, that frankly were her right
to do so. She wasn't disrespectful at all toward her grandfather and the
thought that her grandmother had left her the home was a beautiful
gift. How exciting to be able to have a home and move your family into
this home, with all the visions of the future.

Harvey was bitter but he was not really the main problem and my
client felt that she could handle him being in the home and sharing
space. She knew that sooner or later he would tire, or her grandmother
would dominate him with her love and things would calm down. It
was the shadow man that concerned her and truly I understood her
concerns.

I had to take a break a bit after Sam revealed to me who he was.
I just needed to search deep within myself that ability to truly be

compassionate to what I would consider a monster. During this time, my client was also making changes in the home that I had suggested. Often, our home can get away from us. The daily chores and hard work it takes to tend to a home, work and family can be very tiring and we get behind and then you add on top of all this activity in the home happening, well it is easy to get run down. I wanted my client to take charge a bit, and sort of do an inventory of the home. Clean out old stuff and clutter and revive it a bit. Get back to the family they were and resist the energies of the home. This is a bit hard to really explain, but we can either run from fear or we can face it, and this was a time to take charge. I would do my part and she would do hers, because the reality is that if we must flush this man out, it will take the owner's energy as much as mine to do so. Simple terms imagine some person moving into your home without your permission and you try to get them to leave in all the diplomatic ways possible. If they are not going to leave, then you are faced with that question, can you make them? Can you take charge of yourself and your home?

This allowed me time to also think of my own taking charge of this energy. It did not take me long to come to terms with the fact that I could be that person, that person who could help even the monsters of the world. My job was to help that spirit let go of the sins, the life they lived, all of it, the pain, sorrow, resentment and every human emotion that bound them to that body and allow themselves the forgiveness to ascend in the spirit world. It isn't my forgiveness after all, it is the human spirit that needs to forgive themselves and if that is not going to happen, then I also knew that I would take on the house and deal with pushing him out for the safety of my client and her family.

As I prepared to return, I got a phone call from my client. She asked me if it was possible that some of what I was tuning into in the home was in fact something horrific that was occurring. Of course, that is possible. She went on to explain to me that her wife's ex-husband had been arrested on child pornography. Of course, you can imagine the shock and horror of all this and the very fact that her children have a spirit lurking in the home with this mentality. It was such a blow. This was a time to allow the family to deal with the turn of events that were occurring.

We took a long break from this case. This was a time that the house seemed to cooperate with my wishes and the homes owners wish. Things calmed down as they healed and continued many remodeling of the home. This was when things sort of began to heal for themselves to some degree.

People often ask me if spirits are attracted to certain living beings and I always answer yes of course they are. As I explained early on, our energy and character can totally attract living people and those who have passed. We can be vulnerable during difficult times in our lives to the deceased as much as the living and we must always be aware of this. When your home emits love and tranquility, strength and joy, spirits that vibrate in a lower frequency or negative emotions will not feel comfortable in that space. Now this does not mean that if you have spirits lingering around your home that you have issues within yourself. Do not get me wrong, it just means that if you do have stress in the home or if there are changes in the environment or possible emotional situations occurring, well it can attract energies to you. Hence, why I always say to not do any kind of communications within your home.

My client's home for now is good and everyone is co-existing and building their family unit again as it once was. I wish to return to the home and check in but must be respectful of the appropriate time to do so and when that is possible, I will be there for them.

Below are pictures from the TV show; My Ghost Story, which featured my client's case on one of their Bio Channel TV Episode.

Karen Tatro

Nicole Tatro

The Man that Walks the Barns

Private Case
East Kingston, NH

East Kingston Farm

He came around the corner of the barn looking like a character out of a western cowboy movie. A long dark jacket that lay well below his waist, heavy boots on, and a tall hat. My intuitive eye caught sight of him before my physical eyes did. As I turned to look at where my attention was drawing me, there he was with shotgun in hand aiming at something unseen. The vision, so vivid it caused me to duck. Holy shit, who the hell is that? And just like that he vanished into the thin air.

I came to the beautiful home of a client, who happened to own a thriving therapeutic riding business. Her property was vast with rolling green fields, utility barns and horse stalls full of so many majestic horses. Her property was just alive with people coming and going, partaking in the daily regimen of tending to a busy horse farm. The owner was not at all afraid of her property, more so welcomed the spirits that she felt were lingering and making themselves known to her borders. She was familiar with the spirit world and being a sensitive person herself with many abilities, she was not alarmed one bit, and was quite aware of her spirit "friends' ', she called them. Her horse boarders, however, were not always so comfortable and she felt that she needed to have some clarity of who was haunting her property. She wanted to at least be able to name the spirits that were making themselves known, to help ease the concerns of any riders. The horses themselves did not seem to be bothered by the spirits, she felt they were pretty aware, if not more comfortable with the spirits than some of the riders themselves. She asked me to come check out her farm and help shed some light.

I arrived on a nice sunny late afternoon. The farm was quieting down from a busy day. Everyone knew I was coming and did not mind me one bit, as I strolled the long stalls, pausing now and again with the horses for a quick stroke of their mains. They are such beautiful animals and often find it quite fascinating that I do believe I have a spirit guide as a horse, a black stallion that often comes to me during my galleries and readings to share information for my clients. I used to think that my clients have horse guides, and maybe they do, but I have recently discovered that in fact this may be one of my many spirit guides that works with me.

There was a time when I was around 19ish, that my mom took me to see a medium in NY, while visiting family. This was a woman that she saw on occasion when visiting family that lived in Syracuse. The woman was elderly and blind. She sat in the corner of her room, and motioned us to come in. I was nervous and do not really remember a lot of the reading. What I do remember quite well, was her looking at me with her third eye, and saying, "wow my dear, you have many stars around you. More than I have seen in a long time. She went on to start naming many of them and for the life of me, do you think I would have remembered the names. She said to not be alarmed, as they are spirits that walk with me, and I have a lot of them, some 20 she estimated. I of course was a bit like, okay, I guess, but when she said, one of them is Ida and she wants you to know that she hears you honey, and she is always there. Now this made me begin to cry hysterically, as this was my paternal grandmother; Ida Petrocci. My grandmother was a woman that I was deeply connected with and can honestly say, yes, she walks with me to this very day. There was a time that I did not feel her presence, possibly being busy, or maybe she had other places to visit, but she has become quite known over the years to many of my guests in my paranormal lectures. She often spells her name out when I talk about who she is and how the dowsing rods work. I have heard her voice and seen her beautiful face from time to time, comforting me and that inner knowing that she is a woman who shares my soul on some level.

The Black Stallion, I am not fully sure who is and often spirit guides that walk with us, we are not aware of their identity. This we will discuss another day as that can talk up a whole topic. There is so much wisdom and knowledge that I could share here but chose to keep this more about my spirit tales with my cases.

The horses just watched me as I wandered around the farm. The farm had a lot of energy lurking about, and I could feel torn in many different directions. I went into one of the tack rooms and was welcomed by this cowboy man, as I had described him. Upon better look, it was not so much that he was a cowboy, but more that he wore a long professional business jacket with long coat tails hanging below. He stood in the corner, his dark jacket and hat just light enough to describe. He was tall and thin and stood with pride. I could feel this man's pride a mile long. It surrounded him. He had what looked like a large mustache. I could not quite tell if it was a mustache or goatee, but it covered his entire mouth area. He was charming in his energy and I felt like he wanted to lead me around and listen to all he wanted to share.

This man truly felt like he had an ownership to the property and a man who was well versed in hard work. He accomplished much in his life and had a lot to do with the town. He told me that he had a real connection to the town and how it ran and was supported by him.

What always fascinates me is how connected some of these spirits are to the property they haunt. I felt this man truly did and was so eager to tell me all that he could. He walked the property often and really admired the horse farm. He found it intriguing and unique, being a man who himself was fascinated by how things worked. He worked hard in his life and had to make a name for himself. He said he came from a large family, and somehow took over this property but not in a traditional way, meaning inherited it. He said he saved it, took it over and made it successful. He was a man I felt had a lot of admiration for the farm and personally gave my client advice on looking beyond the box for help in making it even more successful. He helps her, watches her and the staff and this feeling like if he were still alive, he would be there working the land with her.

Spirits often do this and remember their main way of communicating is through telepathy, so often when someone is around spirits for any length of time, well, it only makes sense if the spirit is trying to talk to you, you may in fact have these thoughts and intuitions that you are not sure where they are coming from. My clients had told me she at times seemed to feel that the property talked to her. She even referred to feelings during times when business was hard, the property seemed to always know, and new borders would come, and new opportunities would somehow show up to help get her back on track.

This spirit man had feelings of worry regarding his wife. He indicated that his wife was also here, and he was confused as to why she was so lost and wandering. He worried for her mental health and this caused her loneliness. He loved and adored her.

I felt he was an inventor. He was continually trying to show me different kinds of machines, but I could not fully grasp what they were.

As I left the tack room I continued to wander around. I was greeted by another man who had had many health issues in his body which hurt him physically. He walked with a bit of a hunch and a bit of weight to him. My body felt sore and tired and he was often out of breath. He worked on the property and had connections to it, but the whole horse thing was not really his calling. He often observes and tries to not scare the horses, but he does. He had a sincerity about him and really tried to not scare the horse and chuckled a bit as he was a bit scared of them if truth be told. At one point I heard the name George and I always get so excited when I hear names because normally I do not. I tend to just log it in my brain and if it comes up as a real name, well that is like getting a big fat ice cream cone on a hot day. LOL

I then met the woman who roams the property often lost in thought. She was so distant and comes and goes, almost like she is searching and wandering. It broke my heart a bit as she passed by me, and I felt a sadness deep within her. Finally, she drew closer to me and I saw her as a young woman, not much older than her 20's or 30's. She was well dressed in a pale-yellow dress that lay at her feet. Her hair was sort of partially pulled up and looked like some of it lay down her shoulders. She had lost a child, and this was her mourning. I personally could not fully grasp all that I was feeling within her and found myself getting tired. I wondered if she had poisoned herself. I followed her as she walked out into the field behind the large barn and then slowly laid down in the tall grass, far off in the distance. I got the feeling that is where she was found.

Dark Figure at the end of barn

I then proceeded to the office, which was crazy with energy, but not energy that was easily read. It felt like a lot of residual energy and at first, I thought maybe there was an old foundation underneath. It is hard to describe to people but there is this feeling of knowing where death had happened, and the office felt like something or someone had died there. It was so strong. As I sat in this area for a bit, an animal spirit began to say it had been slaughtered there. I could not tell exactly which animal it was, but images of it along with others being rounded up in some sort of slaughter episode. This all was just coming to me in quick pictures. This property was just so alive with so many different spirits that I was feeling that I will truly have my work cut out for me to fully understand all that is happening here.

As I stood looking out the window from the office, which looks out at the center entrance of the farm and the fields that surround the property. I felt so drawn to the dirt road that led out into the woods. I was drawn there many times during my time walking the property. The feeling of a spirit standing behind me, tickling my sensations. An Indian came forward and although he was so strong in talking, he was talking in his language and I had to sort of get the feeling of what he was saying. This was an area they corralled the animals. He lived on this property and he along with other Indians were here on the property. There were more in the fields, and he stated they were sharing this land. He was very vocal that he was staying connected to the land. His heart and soul were here, and he was never leaving. He told me to tell the woman, which I feel was my client, to build or place totems on the property to help honor and protect the land. He was bothered that there were no markers or honor of their existence. I totally felt honored to have this native man talking to me and truly hung on every word that I could understand. I told him that I would let her know.

There were children on the property as well, one of which indicated he was Rufus's son. He was a delightful young boy and seemed to play in barns and all over the property.

At one point the main male spirit stood behind me and told me that his property was vast and the corner spot, where the road went and I was drawn to, was in fact his homestead. I heard him say the house faced the creek or some sort of body of water. I also felt so drawn to the upper left corner of the property, which later my client told me was a cemetery.

The Cemetery had its own energy about it. Off in the distance there were groups of people standing at the top of the hill, dressed in older style clothing, long coats and dresses with an old style, almost puritan style hats on. It was hard to fully describe. This is one of the most frustrating things about being a medium. I wish I could see super clear and wish I could draw and sketch what I see. Maybe someday I will take a drawing class and try to develop that ability, but for now, I must do the best I can to describe what I see.

What I found so interesting with my client's property was that it seemed to overlap with time. When you think of a home, and all the different people that live in a home, people who raise a family and then move out to have another family move in and they have their own lives to live and their own energy and experiences to infuse into the walls, well it makes me think of how this property had this also in spirit. So it had Native American spirits that seemed to be all in the woods surrounding the fields, spirits of people who lived possibly in the home or in the old homestead that was someplace in the back part of the property. Old heritage of maybe puritan time or some sort of religious group maybe? But that was also overlapping on the land and animals that were part of some sort of slaughtering. What a place to figure out.

On our second visit, the owner informed us that she had done some research and talked to the neighbors, who apparently owned the second home of who she thinks I am connecting with. She pulled out the picture of who she thinks is the main spirit man.

My eyes lit up when I saw the picture. Mr. Rufus Brown. The mustache totally gave it away. It was a signature for sure on his face.

She had told me that his original homestead was in fact deep in the back area of the woods, down that dirt road that I was pointing to. He then built a grander home at the corner of the property, just next to her home. The property was all owned by him and a few homes, along with my client's home and barns were all built on his original property.

This was so exciting. We actually had a ball that night. The owner was open to having me bring groups of people to come investigate with me. We explored the woods on 4 wheelers and whoever did not fit on a 4-wheeler, she loaded them in her pickup truck and off into the woods we went, in search of the foundation of the old homestead.

The homestead was overgrown, but you could see the original stone foundation. It was such a fun night of exploration, laughter and good times.

Rufus Brown, son of Abraham and Betsey Brown, was
born in East Kingston, N. H., June 23,1812.

Rufus Brown had an extremely limited opportunity for education,
but this never stood in his way as a noticeably young entrepreneur.
When he was about fourteen, he began to accompany his uncle, Abel
Brown, a book publisher of Exeter. He traveled the country and assisted
in his auctions of his works. This gave him a practical business education
of the best kind for him, as experience and observation were his best
teachers. His brother Abraham also worked alongside him with his

uncle. After the death of Abel, Rufus and his brother purchased his uncle's estate and continued the business.

Abraham was responsible for the office duty, and Rufus attended to the traveling and sales. All these years he was on the farm with his father whenever business slackened or need for his help was urgent. After closing the publishing, Rufus started dabbling with patents, first taking a washing-machine, next a thrashing-machine, both of which he owned, manufactured, sold machines, and " rights." He continued in this for two years.

Before he was of age he began lumbering. Having accumulated some fourteen hundred dollars by sticking to business and the old home, after caring for his parents, he conceived the idea of making some money in real estate, and when the city of Lawrence, Mass., was laid out, and when the whole place was a waste field, and the dam furnishing the water-power was only in process of construction, and there were no streets there, he began dealing in lots, buying, selling, building, and renting, and by sound judgment and shrewdness was quite successful.

For a time, he engaged in the grocery trade, but only for about a year. Still holding onto his real estate and his tenements, in 1852 he moved to Concord, N. H., as a contractor in the iron-shops of New Hampshire State prison, under Wardens Dow and Webster.

He stayed three years, making general machinery, steel springs, axles, etc. Returning then to his ancestral home in East Kingston, he devoted himself to farming and the improvement of his farmland, that had been heretofore waste and unproductive, was brought rapidly into productive meadow, fields were cleared of their encumbering stone, which furnished material for strong walls, and his example in this direction became of benefit to others. He also thoroughly renovated and repaired and almost rebuilt the dwelling occupied by five generations, and made it the pleasant place that it is to this day.

Rufus resided here until his death. He was representative farmer, not ashamed but justly proud of his avocation, and the care of his estate, with his other diversified business.

He worked hard and took care of his home. A man of vigorous health and active temperament, he was never idle. He worked his land himself, and believed, "he who by the plow would thrive, himself must either hold or drive."

He also was quite gifted in working the machinery on the farm, and brought to use the first mower in the town and was quick to observe and turn to utility any labor-saving inventions. His farm consisted of one hundred acres. Rufus at the age of just twenty-two years old he became a selectman. To be quite honest, Rufus was truly a man of the people, and a typical New England farmer, who has made more than " two blades of grass" grow where only one grew before.

Rufus married Harriet S., daughter of Amos Bacheldor, of East Kingston. Harriet died on March 15, 1846. She was just twenty-nine years of age. He then married his second wife, Ann, on March 12, 1851. Ann died Sept. 14, 1875, aged sixty-three.

It absolutely amazed me to learn all this about Rufus and the fact that on my first day visiting the farm, how delighted he was to have me listen to him. Each time I have gone to the farm, he grabs my ear and wants me to stroll with him. This man is here to stay and incredibly happy with his farm and all the accomplishments of his time, but truly he also is quite impressed with my client's hard work as well. He passed on advice to her during one of our visits and told her specific things to do to help her business succeed. What an amazing gift that is for her to have her land genuinely cared for by the spirit of Mr. Rufus Brown.

We also learned that Mr. Brown donated money to the town upon his death to educate the children. His money was used to build a large brick building in town, which was run as the local elementary school and now is the current home of the Town Hall and offices. As I drive past this building with the large word, "Brown" carved in stone for all to see, I smile and tip my imaginary hat to him. It's an honor to have met him.

I also learned that the tie of the property to Native American lore also was evident. I came across this article in one of my searches of the property and area. Could this be the battle that seemed to take place on the land?

June 23rd of 1710, a party of Abenaki ambushed settlers in East Kingston, N.H. Two settlers were killed and two were taken hostage. There were also several references of battles over the land between the white man and the native. What we also discovered is that there were

7 different tribes that could be tied to that area of East Kingston; Algonquin, Abenaki, Pennacooks, Piscataqua, Pequawkets, Squamscot, and Winnecowet.

This was also a time where the existence of religious communities was also making themselves known and battling over the land. There was reference by the neighbor who just happens to live in Mr. Brown's beautiful Victorian home, that the Mormons were visitors of the cemetery on the hill. The Cemetery had many ancestors of the Mormon church. Could this be the groups of people we were often seeing with the long dresses and coats and hats.

The neighbor, Joe Freeman, helped validate with my client that his grandfather was George Freeman who I described in detail, along with others who I had brought to the farm. He had said that his grandfather had bought the Victorian home from Rufus's home, and made it into a successful cattle farm during his time. This was the man who walked the property and tried to not scare the horses. This was very touching for us all as well as the neighbors to think that their grandfather also was checking in on his property. They have also had experiences in their home, which one day we will make those arrangements to pay a visit. I can only speculate that Mr. Brown and Mr. Freeman will be felt there as well.

The neighbor also informed us that Mr. Rufus Brown's original homestead back in the wooded area was several different businesses in its day. He referred that it was a tavern and brothel at one time as well. Quite interesting really and not surprising at all.

What is sad to think is that Mr. Rufus himself did not live to be an old man and possibly that is why he still walks the property and the barns. Dying in his 60's was quite a shock as for so many that is when you are in your prime of life. This man had worked hard since he was 14 years old, making his way in life to learn all he could and created quite a name for himself and successful endeavors. When he was able to maybe sit back and let the farm run itself, but he would never do that, this I know. These kinds of men do not retire, they don't soak up all the rewards, they probably know they will have plenty of time to sleep when they are buried in the ground and they take their last breath. I chuckle as I type this, because even in his afterlife, I feel he is still working.

The Mystery Girl

Private Case
Jaffrey, N.H.

One of the most bizarre cases I worked on and truly have to say still to this day makes me just question how much our energy is in the things we own and the things we touch and interact with. As I had said before that possibly our DNA is scattered along the way, in the crevices of a home or places we spend a great deal of time in, and who is to say that a medium or sensitive person comes along and awakens us in some unique way? Or is it possible that all our information and our very existence is stored in that DNA particle that is left behind?

I was asked to go to a home in Jaffrey, N.H. which is not too far from my hometown. It was quite the beautiful estate, with a lavish garden area, and rolling fields that seemed to go for miles. This case I cannot share the details as it was very private and the family was asking me to come and assess the property as they were going to be putting it on the market and wanted to make sure it was not going to be a problem for any future buyers. The estate had been in the family and the father of the family had recently passed, leaving the estate to settle among the children. There were some indications that the estate was haunted, and the assistant wanted to have it thoroughly gone through. She knew the owner and many relatives were still wandering the home and many had reached out to her, which was partly the reason she wanted it fully checked out. I think for many of us, there is a time that validation is so important.

I spent several visits in the home and yes, there were a few family members at the locations. The owner of the home followed me around, as they often do and told me a great deal of things that were unsettling to him. This man did not expect to pass and was truly building a home that he had wanted to be his personal retreat. His heart and soul were into this home and the thought of his grown children arguing over the estate was one thing, but the fact that not one of them really seemed to even care about it. All they wanted was the money from the sale of the home, and the items of the home and the rich character that it had, was of little interest to them. I felt awful for this man, he absolutely loved this home and his property and was quite willing to give it to his assistant if he had known it was going to be up for sale. His wife was overwhelmed with the arguing and in many ways was bullied a bit by the adult children. My job was to ensure that the house would not have any paranormal issues.

As I walked the huge estate, I came to the top floor which had several exceptionally large bedrooms for guests and a long hallway. There was a sort of common center area that had many boxes and items that seemed to indicate family decorations for holidays and storage bins full of pictures and such.

As I came to the last bedroom, the room sort of took on an energy of its own. I felt very much like the room swirled with energy and had a bit of a time clearing my thoughts. I didn't like the feel of this room at all. I went to the window and just stared out into the beautiful patio below. The day was breathtaking, with the sun shining and a warm breeze. Within a few moments I was aware of a young woman behind me. I let her come into my view and realized that she was quite young, not a teenager but more of a young woman in her early 20's possibly. Her hair was long and stringy, laying down both sides of her face. She was so distraught looking and not a very warm and fuzzy feeling about her at all. She was just staring at me and then the next thing shocked the hell out of me and the only way I can describe it is from a horror movie. Imagine your head suddenly shaking violently side to side like a video was fast forwarding the movement. Her head was shaking so violently and fast that I thought, what the hell am I seeing. It was quite startling and made me step back a bit. She was clearly presenting like she was insane and, in an asylum, based on how her head and body were moving. Something right out of a horror movie.

I took a breath and started to talk to her and explain why I was there. She began to show me some imagery and I knew that she had mental issues and seemed to have been kept restrained and awful things were done to her. I felt that she needed me to see these things and part of her was wanting, again to just be heard. I listened and talked to her but truthfully, I did most of the talking because I felt she was not able to fully understand all I was saying. So, I just sat with her and tried to calm her energy as best I could. What was very odd to me was that this woman was not from the house and I could feel it. She did not feel like she belonged, and I truly was not sure who she was, and I kept hearing that she was brought here, and she did not know where she was. She told me her name was Mary. That totally shocked me because as I said before, I do not often hear names.

I had the privilege of having the assistant a phone call away and she knew the entire family's history and family tree. I quickly called her to see if this was a family member and if she had any knowledge of a woman fitting this description. She did not but did express that she also had a hard time on that floor but never knew why. The thing with this home was that I was not going to have the time to fully research and spend multiple visits at. Time was of the essence and I knew that I had to figure this out quickly.

I went back upstairs and just sat for a moment letting my own senses talk to me and as I got up and found myself walking back and forth in the hallway, thinking okay why am I walking back and forth in this hallway? Was this something she did? Was this a path of some sort? I stopped at a picture on the wall that caught my attention. It was not a picture but a piece of woven material that was framed. As I got closer to it, it had stitch work of flowers and intricate designs, all detailed and beautifully crafted. The more I looked at it, omg, there was a name stitched in the center of the design. A woman's full name, date of birth and date of death. The first name was Mary, and she was 29 years old. MARY! The more I looked at it, the reality hit me that it wasn't a thread that was stitched so intricately in the material but HAIR! It was hair! This was the freakiest thing ever and I immediately called the assistant to ask her about this. She said that so many of the items in areas of the home were bought at auctions and antique dealers to replicate the time period they wanted to have when decorating each floor and room of the estate. She didn't have knowledge of the item I was referring to, but she knew it was bought and hung up along with all the décor. This home was just the owner's private get away, and not their main estate, so all the items in the home were not original family heirlooms.

So, it hit me that this picture frame was bought some place and hung on the wall in this home and this young woman Mary's spirit was traveling with her hair. As bizarre as that sounds, upon doing some research this was a common practice in certain time periods. We mourn our loved ones in many ways I suppose, but boy this was sure a surprise to me.

I had many thoughts going through my mind as I thought, how can this be? How can this spirit of this girl be trapped or more so bound by her hair in this woven tribute to her life? I can only imagine that at one time, those who loved this young lady, wanted to keep her with them always and possibly a mother mourning the loss of her daughter. The loss of a loved one is something we all will experience in our lives and I cannot judge how people mourn as we all must make peace with that heartbreak. I can understand that a parent would want to hold onto mementos and trinkets and property that would be reminders of those we lost. I can honestly imagine even keeping our loved one's room the same and wanting to smell their scent on their clothing to truly ease the pain. I have done so many readings and galleries with clients who have lost their children and it is brutal, the raw emotions and pain they feel. I have often driven home from a gallery hysterically crying and letting go of all that I absorbed from these clients. I feel for them and can't imagine being in their shoes. So here I am with a piece of this young lady's essence, the very thought of it is as touching and bizarre all in the same.

I went back into the room and validated best I could and realized that at this moment, proving who this young woman was, well, it was irrelevant. What mattered is that she found peace and to unbind her from this piece. I helped her find her way and restored the energy flow of the room and area.

Over the years I have wandered into antique shops and do have to say that some of them have that familiar feeling. The knowing that spirits of people are bonded to their favorite piece of furniture or treasure that once had special meaning for them. At a gallery one evening in Leominster, MA this same occurrence happened. As I was describing a spirit to the group of ladies, no one in the room could identify the older man coming through. After a few moments, when I saw him standing next to the salon's front desk which was very old and quite antique looking, the owner spoke up and asked if it was possible that I would be tuning into the man who owned that very desk? She happened to know the man and when he passed, she had gone to the estate sale and bought the desk. She did not think of it when I was describing him as she was thinking of it being family members coming in for the guests, and not a total stranger. But she said I described him exactly as he was, and he was standing next to his very desk. How bizarre that was again to realize that this is totally possible. This man was not stuck with his desk, but he was just touching base and dropping in to say hello.

I did an event several years ago with Brian Cano from the TV show Haunted Collector, which was based totally on discovering haunted items causing the paranormal activity in homes. They would find the source of the haunting and remove the item to have the paranormal activity often cease. Quite interesting it all is.

So when you shop in antique stores and certain pieces call to you, stop for a moment and follow your intuition as to whether it is your interest in the item that is calling you, the perfect great find, or if it is a spirit calling to you.

As I conclude this first book in the series, I want to thank everyone for being a part of my journey. Thank you all for following me along the way of understanding my mediumship. I love hosting events for so many reasons, one being the opportunity to explore and the second is to help others have those profound awakenings themselves. Spirits have a great deal to teach us in this life. You see, at some point we all share the same common thread that is woven within each of us, death. We all are born and we all will die someday. We have come a long way in our education of the process and so much science and study in the medical field can only tell us so much. Sooner or later we will experience it for ourselves and be on the other side, the side we may have quick visions of and thoughts and insights about, but we will never fully know until that moment. Spirits, however, are there in that afterlife and can share and tell us about not only where they are, but also their viewpoint of living and dying. Understanding their viewpoint, their experiences, and their insight to what holds them back, what scares them or keeps them from finding peace, truly is wisdom for us to learn from so that we do not make those mistakes. To heal our insecurities, our inner struggles, our fears and regrets, while we are living. I always say, learn from the source and you have a far better chance of knowing the truth.

Enjoy!

Spirit Adventures (book two), to be continued...

Messages from the Spirit

"I have come too many to share with humanity. You cannot follow me from a book, nor can you follow the preacher, the preacher, the preacher does not change people. Experience and compassion are the tools, and they are in you once you see! I am in you and not outside of you. Do not lose faith for I am here for you. I can guide you, but you must lead your own way."

"See the higher picture or vision of yourself. What more can you be? What more can you inspire? Many are here to just be and live a robotic life, experiencing the playground but never fully experiencing all the playground that life has to offer. Wake up to your higher life."

"Our gifts as Divine Beings! Each Soul has many layers of existence and each has places yet to discover. What lies within the Soul can only be decoded from the Soul's Core. However, it can be 'felt', in a human way. It can be felt through the Heart. The Pureness of Love. The Pureness of Being."

"My Children you are not broken. Hardships and pain are not meant to break you. They are living. See the joy in all that transpires in life; the good and the bad. For there is purpose for all things and it is part of your development. Honor that you are a Spiritual Being, each and every one of you and all those living."

"Seek and you shall find what is always said my Children, but when you learn to not seek, only then will you find what you desire. When the question is asked, the answer is lost. For only when the question doesn't exist is it found. Stop wasting time on the search, the solution and resolution is as simple as stating; "I am". For what you believe to be true is. So, create and re-create your belief. You are a composite of all your experiences and beliefs."

Some Cool Pictures of Evidence

The Conjuring House Investigation

We captured this Shadow Person in the basement of who we believe is a little boy that we were communicating with that evening and has made himself known each visit.

Dark Shadow on Daniel's Arm

There was a spirit man in the corner who was getting very impatient with Daniel taking my attention. We did not notice the picture until after reviewing our photos.

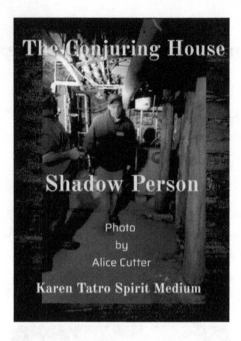

Spirit Orb of a man I was seeing in the corner area of the basement at the Shanley Hotel.

Miss Maggie our beloved cat of 15 years. I felt her visiting one day while enjoying our two new kitties, and there she was! This is classic spirit energy!

Spirit Orb of a man standing in the corner

Miss Maggie our beloved cat. I felt her on the bed one day and took this picture

White Mist forming at the Shanley Hotel/Bright Light

   Pay attention to the dresser in the mirror. I could feel the woman
in the room that mirror is showing. She was not wanting to come out
of the room. I took a series of pictures and you will see this white mist
forming.

White Mist fully covering the dresser!

This is one of my favorite pictures. This white mist has shown up on many of my photos from the Shanley Hotel and only in the Bordello area. I have not been able to figure out what the light is in the room. There was not a lamp or any other light source turned on in this room. This is a classic Spirit Energy.

About the Author

Karen Tatro lives in N.H with her husband, Steve and children; Nicole and Garrett. From the time she was a small child, Karen has had a deep connection with the spirit world. She could see, hear, and feel the presence of spirits and knew that, beyond her intellect; the Divine Spirit world existed and was all around. Growing up as a sensitive, she often describes her life as having, "one foot on Earth and one in the Clouds". Karen embraces and shares her abilities with people for the purpose of inspiration, wisdom, education, and healing. Tatro's credentials and abilities in the paranormal field have led her to appear on two national TV shows dealing with paranormal content: Syfy Channel's Ghost Hunters TAPS, and the Biography Channel's My Ghost Story. WMUR Channel 9 news had interviewed and filmed Karen while she and her partner Brian Cano of Haunted Collector investigated the Ellacoya Country Store in Gilford, N.H in 2014. She has also held paranormal events with a few of the Celebrity Ghost Hunters such as Amy Bruni and Steve Gonsalves. She has been featured on several New Hampshire radio stations, including WOKQ 95.7 where she was interviewed regarding the famously "caught on video" ghost at the small Gilford store.

Tatro is also a published author of a children's book, "I'm a Super Hero~I'm not Afraid of Ghosts!" It's a wonderful book for families who have children of all ages that are sensitive and afraid of their bedrooms at night; afraid of ghosts and things they might sense but cannot see or quite understand.

She is a Paranormal & Spiritual event Host for the general public, holding monthly investigations at the famously known; Conjuring House in R. I., a location that has become a movie franchise based on the case files of Ed and Lorraine Warren. She holds public events which allows people to explore these amazing locations and understand their own abilities and interest in the paranormal field. She also travels throughout the New England states, holding private mediumship galleries in private homes for small gatherings. Karen will deliver messages from passed loved ones, and spirit guides to the guests in the group. Karen also offers online readings and Rune Stone readings.

All information can be found on her website; www.karentatro.com

Karen is currently working on a TV Pilot featuring he work as a medium.